Francis Frith's

THE WEST MIDLANDS

PHOTOGRAPHIC MEMORIES

Francis Frith's
WEST MIDLANDS

Clive Hardy

First published in the United Kingdom in 2000 by
Frith Book Company Ltd

Paperback Edition 2000
ISBN 1-85937-289-9

Hardback Reprinted in 2000
ISBN 1-85937-109-4

British Library Cataloguing in Publication Data

Francis Frith's
The West Midlands
Clive Hardy

Frith Book Company Ltd
Frith's Barn, Teffont,
Salisbury, Wiltshire SP3 5QP
Tel: +44 (0) 1722 716 376
Email: info@frithbook.co.uk
www.frithbook.co.uk

Printed and bound in Great Britain

As with any historical database the Frith archive is constantly being corrected and improved and the publishers would welcome information on omissions or inaccuracies

Contents

Francis Frith: Victorian Pioneer 7

Frith's Archive - A Unique Legacy 10

The West Midlands - An Introduction 12

The Black Country 18

Around Birmingham 56

Around Coventry 89

Other Places 105

Index 115

Free Mounted Print Voucher 119

FRANCIS FRITH: *Victorian Pioneer*

FRANCIS FRITH, Victorian founder of the world-famous photographic archive, was a complex and multitudinous man. A devout Quaker and a highly successful Victorian businessman, he was both philosophic by nature and pioneering in outlook.

By 1855 Francis Frith had already established a wholesale grocery business in Liverpool, and sold it for the astonishing sum of £200,000, which is the equivalent today of over £15,000,000. Now a multi-millionaire, he was able to indulge his passion for travel. As a child he had pored over travel books written by early explorers, and his fancy and imagination had been stirred by family holidays to the sublime mountain regions of Wales and Scotland. 'What a land of spirit-stirring and enriching scenes and places!' he had written. He was to return to these scenes of grandeur in later years to 'recapture the thousands of vivid and tender memories', but with a different purpose. Now in his thirties, and captivated by the new science of photography, Frith set out on a series of pioneering journeys to the Nile regions that occupied him from 1856 until 1860.

INTRIGUE AND ADVENTURE

He took with him on his travels a specially-designed wicker carriage that acted as both dark-room and sleeping chamber. These far-flung journeys were packed with intrigue and adventure. In his life story, written when he was sixty-three, Frith tells of being held captive by bandits, and of fighting 'an awful midnight battle to the very point of surrender with a deadly pack of hungry, wild dogs'. Sporting flowing Arab costume, Frith arrived at Akaba by camel seventy years before Lawrence, where he encountered 'desert princes and rival sheikhs, blazing with jewel-hilted swords'.

During these extraordinary adventures he was assiduously exploring the desert regions bordering the Nile and patiently recording the antiquities and peoples with his camera. He was the first photographer to venture beyond the sixth cataract. Africa was still the mysterious 'Dark Continent', and Stanley and Livingstone's historic meeting was a decade into the future. The conditions for picture taking confound belief. He laboured for hours in his wicker dark-room in the sweltering heat of the desert, while the volatile chemicals fizzed dangerously in their trays. Often he was forced to work in remote tombs and caves where conditions were cooler. Back in London he exhibited his photographs and was 'rapturously cheered' by members of the Royal Society. His reputation as a photographer was made overnight. An eminent modern historian has likened their impact on the population of the time to that on our own generation of the first photographs taken on the surface of the moon.

Venture of a Life-Time

Characteristically, Frith quickly spotted the opportunity to create a new business as a specialist publisher of photographs. He lived in an era of immense and sometimes violent change. For the poor in the early part of Victoria's reign work was a drudge and the hours long, and people had precious little free time to enjoy themselves.

Most had no transport other than a cart or gig at their disposal, and had not travelled far beyond the boundaries of their own town or village. However, by the 1870s, the railways had threaded their way across the country, and Bank Holidays and half-day Saturdays had been made obligatory by Act of Parliament. All of a sudden the ordinary working man and his family were able to enjoy days out and see a little more of the world.

With characteristic business acumen, Francis Frith foresaw that these new tourists would enjoy having souvenirs to commemorate their days out. In 1860 he married Mary Ann Rosling and set out with the intention of photographing every city, town and village in Britain. For the next thirty years he travelled the country by train and by pony and trap, producing fine photographs of seaside resorts and beauty spots that were keenly bought by millions of Victorians. These prints were painstakingly pasted into family albums and pored over during the dark nights of winter, rekindling precious memories of summer excursions.

The Rise of Frith & Co

Frith's studio was soon supplying retail shops all over the country. To meet the demand he gathered about him a small team of photographers, and published the work of independent artist-photographers of the calibre of Roger Fenton and Francis Bedford. In order to gain some understanding of the scale of Frith's business one only has to look at the catalogue issued by Frith & Co in 1886: it runs to some 670

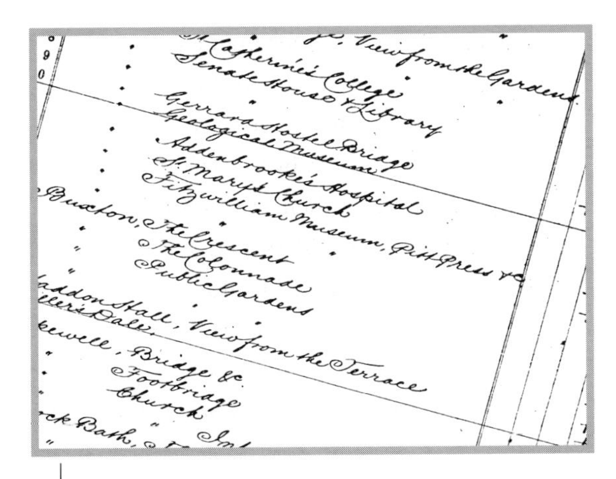
Catherine's College
View from the Gardens
Senate House & Library
Gerrard Hostel Bridge
Geological Museum
Addenbrooke's Hospital
St Mary's Church
Fitzwilliam Museum, Pitt Press &c
Buxton, The Crescent
The Colonnade
Public Gardens
addon Hall, View from the Terrace
kewell, Bridge &c.
Footbridge
Church

pages, listing not only many thousands of views of the British Isles but also many photographs of most European countries, and China, Japan, the USA and Canada – note the sample page shown above from the hand-written *Frith & Co* ledgers detailing pictures taken. By 1890 Frith had created the greatest specialist photographic publishing company in the world, with over 2,000 outlets – more than the combined number that Boots and WH Smith have today! The picture on the right shows the *Frith & Co* display board at Ingleton in the Yorkshire Dales. Beautifully constructed with mahogany frame and gilt inserts, it could display up to a dozen local scenes.

POSTCARD BONANZA

The ever-popular holiday postcard we know today took many years to develop. In 1870 the Post Office issued the first plain cards, with a pre-printed stamp on one face. In 1894 they allowed other publishers' cards to be sent through the mail with an attached adhesive halfpenny stamp. Demand grew rapidly, and in 1895 a new size of postcard was permitted called the court card, but there was little room for illustration. In 1899, a year after Frith's death, a new card measuring 5.5 x 3.5 inches became the standard format, but it was not until 1902 that the divided back came into being, with address and message on one face and a full-size illustration on the other. *Frith & Co* were in the vanguard of postcard development, and Frith's sons Eustace and Cyril continued their father's monumental task, expanding the number of views offered to the public and recording more and more places in Britain, as the coasts and countryside were opened up to mass travel.

Francis Frith died in 1898 at his villa in Cannes, his great project still growing. The archive he created continued in business for another seventy years. By 1970 it contained over a third of a million pictures of 7,000 cities, towns and villages. The massive photographic record Frith has left to us stands as a living monument to a special and very remarkable man.

Frith's Archive: *A Unique Legacy*

Francis Frith's legacy to us today is of immense significance and value, for the magnificent archive of evocative photographs he created provides a unique record of change in 7,000 cities, towns and villages throughout Britain over a century and more. Frith and his fellow studio photographers revisited locations many times down the years to update their views, compiling for us an enthralling and colourful pageant of British life and character.

We tend to think of Frith's sepia views of Britain as nostalgic, for most of us use them to conjure up memories of places in our own lives with which we have family associations. It often makes us forget that to Francis Frith they were records of daily life as it was actually being lived in the cities, towns and villages of his day. The Victorian age was one of great and often bewildering change for ordinary people, and though the pictures evoke an impression of slower times, life was as busy and hectic as it is today.

We are fortunate that Frith was a photographer of the people, dedicated to recording the minutiae of everyday life. For it is this sheer wealth of visual data, the painstaking chronicle of changes in dress, transport, street layouts, buildings, housing, engineering and landscape that captivates us so much today. His remarkable images offer us a powerful link with the past and with the lives of our ancestors.

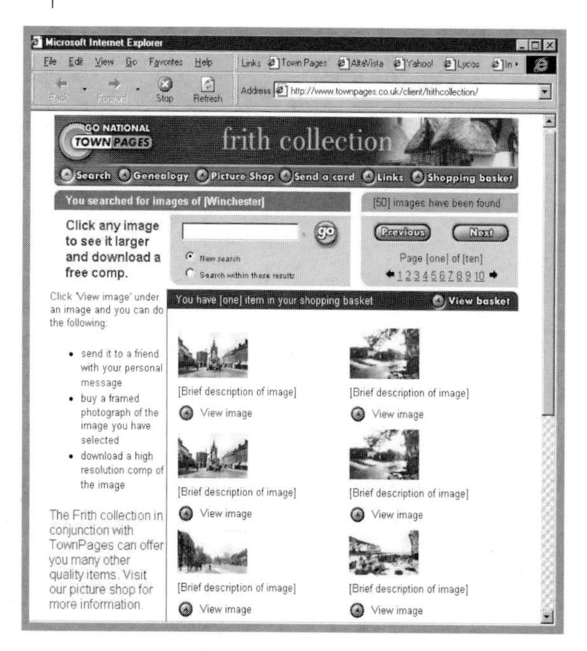

See Frith at www. frithbook.co.uk

Today's Technology

Computers have now made it possible for Frith's many thousands of images to be accessed almost instantly. In the Frith archive today, each photograph is carefully 'digitised' then stored on a CD Rom. Frith archivists can locate a single photograph amongst thousands within seconds. Views can be catalogued and sorted under a variety of categories of place and content to the immediate benefit of researchers. Inexpensive reference prints can be created for them at the touch of a mouse button, and a wide range of books and other printed materials assembled and published for a wider, more general readership - in the next twelve months over a hundred Frith local history titles will be published! The day-to-day workings of the archive are very different from how they were in Francis Frith's time: imagine the herculean task of sorting through eleven tons of glass negatives as Frith had to do to locate a particular sequence of pictures! Yet the archive still prides itself on maintaining the same high standards of excellence laid down by Francis Frith, including the painstaking cataloguing and indexing of every view.

It is curious to reflect on how the internet now allows researchers in America and elsewhere greater instant access to the archive than Frith himself ever enjoyed. Many thousands of individual views can be called up on screen within seconds on one of the Frith internet sites, enabling people living continents away to revisit the streets of their ancestral home town, or view places in Britain where they have enjoyed holidays. Many overseas researchers welcome the chance to view special theme selections, such as transport, sports, costume and ancient monuments.

We are certain that Francis Frith would have heartily approved of these modern developments, for he himself was always working at the very limits of Victorian photographic technology.

The Value of the Archive Today

Because of the benefits brought by the computer, Frith's images are increasingly studied by social historians, by researchers into genealogy and ancestory, by architects, town planners, and by teachers and schoolchildren involved in local history projects. In addition, the archive offers every one of us a unique opportunity to examine the places where we and our families have lived and worked down the years. Immensely successful in Frith's own era, the archive is now, a century and more on, entering a new phase of popularity.

The Past in Tune with the Future

Historians consider the Francis Frith Collection to be of prime national importance. It is the only archive of its kind remaining in private ownership and has been valued at a million pounds. However, this figure is now rapidly increasing as digital technology enables more and more people around the world to enjoy its benefits.

Francis Frith's archive is now housed in an historic timber barn in the beautiful village of Teffont in Wiltshire. Its founder would not recognize the archive office as it is today. In place of the many thousands of dusty boxes containing glass plate negatives and an all-pervading odour of photographic chemicals, there are now ranks of computer screens. He would be amazed to watch his images travelling round the world at unimaginable speeds through network and internet lines.

The archive's future is both bright and exciting. Francis Frith, with his unshakeable belief in making photographs available to the greatest number of people, would undoubtedly approve of what is being done today with his lifetime's work. His photographs, depicting our shared past, are now bringing pleasure and enlightenment to millions around the world a century and more after his death.

WEST MIDLANDS – *An Introduction*

FOR A THOUSAND years our county system had served England well, but in 1974 the Local Government Act 1972 came into effect, and with it a came a radical realignment of many of our county boundaries with scant regard for history, tradition, community or identity. Among the changes, Southern Lancashire was butchered to create the Metropolitan Boroughs of Merseyside and Greater Manchester; Cumberland and Westmorland were abolished altogether; and Rutland, England's smallest county, was dragged kicking and screaming into a merger with Leicestershire. Yorkshire, our largest county, was dissected. The provisions of the Act saw the abolition of the three ridings, an administrative division that had served the county well since the days when it was ruled by its own Scandinavian kings at York. The ridings were replaced by three new counties, North Yorkshire, South Yorkshire and West Yorkshire. In addition former East and West Riding territory was hived off to create something called Humberside; Lancashire and the new county of Cumbria gained parts of the western areas of the West Riding; and a part of the North Riding which included the great steel town of Middlesborough was incorporated into the new county of Cleveland. Staffordshire, Worcestershire and Warwickshire would also be robbed of territory, as the Black Country, Birmingham, and Coventry were transferred into a new county to be known as the West Midlands. Warwickshire came out worse off. At a stroke the county lost not only a large area of territory, but its manufacturing and commercial heartland centred on Birmingham and Coventry.

The book is divided into four sections: the Black Country, Around Birmingham, Around Coventry, and Other Places. Where the Black Country begins and ends has been argued over for decades, but most people accept that it is the 100 square miles or so of territory lying within the quadrilateral Wolverhampton across to Walsall, from Walsall down to Halesowen, across to Stourbridge and back up to Wolverhampton. Those of you with other ideas can fight it out amongst yourselves. Among the places featured in this section are Wolverhampton, Bilston, Walsall, Dudley, Stourbridge and Kingswinford.

The pictures of Wolverhampton were

taken between 1890 and 1910. First mentioned in its own right in 1078 and granted a weekly market in 1258, Wolverhampton was the largest borough in Staffordshire until the creation of the borough of Stoke-on-Trent in 1910. By the early decades of the 19th century access to coal, iron, and the ever expanding canal network gave Wolverhampton a competitive edge. Though famed as the centre for lock-making, the town was heavily engaged in producing a wide range of products including hinges, bolts, screws, edged tools, hammers, fire-irons, candlesticks, buckles and screws. For both home and overseas markets Wolverhampton manufacturers produced tea and coffee pots, tin plate and japanned goods, caddies and inkstands. There were also brass founders, chemical works, a munitions plant, and yarn spinning for woollen carpets. Later, when the railways came, additional jobs were brought to the town with the opening of Stafford Road Works, part of which was built on the site of the original Shrewsbury & Birmingham Railway's terminus of 1849. By the 1890s the town's population was approaching 90,000. One guide book from the period describes Wolverhampton as ' the capital of the Black Country, an extensive coal and iron mining district, in which vegetation is almost entirely replaced by heaps of slag and cinders'.

It is hard, then, to reconcile the fact that in the early 19th century Wolverhampton was still very much a market town, and the best dairy herd in the county belonged to a Mr Miller at Dunstall. Most of his milk production went for cheese, and calves were fattened to eight or ten weeks. Cows too old for the dairy or those accidently barren were fattened for the butcher. In June 1811 Miller sold some cows at Wolverhampton market. One was a six-year-old which had been milked for three summers and had calved once. The cow weighed in at 230lbs per quarter; Miller estimated that she had given sufficient milk for 480lbs of cheese a year, 120lbs of whey butter, and she had given birth to a 120lb calf.

Bilston's associations with coal mining, quarrying, smelting of iron ore, forging and so on are long. There were coal pits during the reign of Edward I, and the Reverend Richard Ames, curate of St Leonard's in the 17th century, wrote in the church register that coal had been got at Bilston since 1380. What we know for certain is that in 1490 William Tomkys, Thomas Jackson and Nycolas Foxall searched for coal in Moorfields. By 1827 Bilston pits were producing 316,000 tonnes of coal a year, thanks to the 30ft seam of Thick Coal; it was near the surface and easily accessible at Tipton and Wednesbury. Bilston had a lock-making industry of sorts in the 16th century but it remained fairly static; along with Pontypool, Bilston was an early centre for japanning - the copying of Japanese goods by English factories.

On the other hand, the earliest that Brierley Hill is known to have been inhabited is 1619, though by the mid 18th century it too was noted for its coal pits, nail-making, brickworks, forges and glass-houses. Brierley's development was influenced by the Stourbridge and Dudley Canals, cut in the 1770s and 1780s to provide Stourbridge glass works with Dudley coal, and with access to other markets by way of a junction with the Staffs & Worcs Canal at Stourton. A further boost came in 1792 with the opening of a link between the Dudley and Birmingham Canals. The major industrial development at Brierley

Hill was building the Earl of Dudley's Round Oak Iron Works in the 1850s. Though by no means the first iron works in the area, it would become the most important. It was constructed on the opposite side of the canal to the New Level Furnaces and adjacent to the tracks of the recently opened Oxford, Worcester & Wolverhampton Railway. Production began at Round Oak in 1857, and as demand grew the works was gradually extended. In 1889 a chain works was commissioned, and in 1892 Round Oak switched over to producing steel. Our pictures of Brierley Hill were taken in the 1960s, a time when Round Oak was one of the most modern steel plants in the West Midlands and capable of producing in excess of 250,000 tonnes a year.

Stourbridge came into existence at a crossing point of the Stour. By the end of the 14th century it had its own market, and during the 16th century refugees from Hungary and Lorraine established a glass industry on Lye Waste, thanks to the quality of the local fireclay. The seams between Stourbridge and Gornalwood would prove to be the most important in the Black Country. Writing in 1817 in his book 'Topographical History of Staffordshire', William Pitt describes Stourbridge fireclay. 'The clay possesses this peculiar excellency, that a pot made of it, with a proper heat, will melt almost anything into glass, provided it be fluxed with proper salts'. Some of these clay pots were huge, holding 1.5 tonnes. Their life span was determined very much by their size, anything from one to twelve months, and a ready supply of quality fireclay on the doorstep would see the glass industry entrenched in the area.

Around Birmingham

Birmingham was first visited by a Frith cameraman in 1890. Redevelopment of the town centre began in the 1850s and continued into the 1880s. It was a two-fold plan. First and foremost it aimed to give Birmingham a grand civic area as befitting one of the country's leading industrial and commercial towns. Among the buildings erected, the Birmingham and Midland Institute, Paradise Street, opened in 1856. Its metallurgical school became one of the most important in the 19th century, and it was also famed for its penny lectures. Among the visiting lecturers were the likes of Charles Dickens, who gave some of his earliest public lectures here to help raise funds for the Institute. Other visitors included T H Huxley and Anthony Trollope. The university, or Mason College as it was then called, was built between 1875-80 at a cost of £60,000 and was endowed by Sir Josiah Mason with a further £140,000. The Grand Hotel, Colmore Row was completed in 1875, the first meeting in the council chamber of the new Council House took place in November 1878, and the Art Gallery and Museum opened in 1885. A school of art was also opened in 1885, and a technical school in 1896. A new County Court building was opened in 1882, and in 1889 Birmingham was elevated to city status. The granting of an Assize was, however, dependent upon the city having suitable courts. Sir Aston Webb and Ingress Bell were commissioned to design the Victoria Law Courts, Corporation Street.

Secondly, redevelopment would rid the town centre of a slum district that covered 93 acres. Joseph Chamberlain introduced improvement schemes - they were badly needed, for between 1871 and 1875 the death rate within the Birmingham slum area was 3.2 per cent above the national average. Health inspectors, recruited in the late 1870s in an effort to raise standards, found that the wells used by 60,000 people in the slum area were contaminated with either raw sewerage or other substances. As befitting Birmingham's status, a new principal thoroughfare was to be driven through the slum area. There would also be a number of new side and connecting streets, such as one from Monmouth Street along the side of St Philip's Church and across Temple Row. A new link would also be cut across John Street to the junction of Dale End and Coleshill Street, while a further link would cut across Little Cherry Street and Crooked Lane to the High Street. If all went well, the unhealthy area of Steelhouse Lane, Lancaster Street, Stafford Street, and Aston Lane from Steelhouse Lane to Costa Green would soon be but a memory. The new street (Corporation Street) itself would rid the town of the evil-smelling and common lodging district around Old Square and Lichfield Street, and provide a much-needed new road out of the centre to the north-east. Of the slum area, Councillor Ward said that 'the rubbish and dilapidation of whole quarters have reminded me of Strasbourg which I saw soon after the bombardment'.

Before Birmingham received its Charter of Incorporation in 1838 it was divided into a number of districts, each of which was controlled by administrators known as Street Commissioners. They had considerable powers: they could levy taxes and appoint bailiffs. There was no audit of their dealings, and they were unaccountable to the public at large; whether or not it is true, many were considered to be corrupt, devious and without scruples - nothing new there. The Commissioners were responsible for such things as street lighting, public works and repairs, and markets. One thing the Street Commissioners did do was to build the covered market hall in Worcester Street. Designed by Charles Edge and costing £67,261, the market opened in November 1834. When our cameraman visited it in 1896 it was normal practice for fishmongers to sell fish such as Dover sole, whiting, and halibut live. On Saturday nights some traders would sell off perishables cheaply to the poor. This could be a bit of a free-for-all; a Mr Mountford, a butcher, said that he often had to defend his wife and himself from 'thugs' when he did it.

By 1906 Birmingham was described as 'the fourth town of England in size and population (522,182 inhabitants in 1901), and the see of an Anglican (since 1905) and of a Roman Catholic bishop, standing on a series of gentle hills in the N W corner of Warwickshire. In plan it is irregular, and many of its older streets are narrow and crooked: but the modern business thoroughfares are broad and handsomely built. It is the chief centre in England, if not the world, of the manufacture of brass, iron, and other metallic wares of all kinds, and it is the most important industrial town in England after Manchester. In spite of its numerous tall chimneys and often smoky atmosphere, Birmingham has the reputation of being healthier than most large manufacturing towns'. What is surprising is that given the conditions prevailing in the slum area there was never a major outbreak of cholera. There were several deaths during an outbreak in 1832, and in July 1865 there were 243 inmates in the local workhouse with symptoms, but all recovered. Outbreaks of smallpox seem to have had higher casualty rates. There was an epidemic in 1884 in which 1591 cases were reported. From among the 1348 patients who had been vaccinated there were 59 deaths, from the unvaccinated 90 deaths, and from the re-vaccinated no deaths.

Around Coventry

The origins of Coventry are obscure, but in all probability it began in the 7th century with the establishment of a hamlet to serve an Anglo-Saxon convent; both were destroyed by the Danes in 1016. In 1043 Leofric, Earl of Mercia, and Lord of Couentrev, founded a Benedictine Priory which he endowed with half his land in the town - hence the division of the town into the Prior's Half and the Earl's Half, the approximate border running through Broadgate. The town itself grew up at the junction of the roads to Warwick, Lichfield, Leicester and London, and its first golden age would dawn during the 14th century.

By this time Coventry's trade was founded on wool, leather goods, metal working, and the manufacture of soap, but cloth was becoming increasingly important. A royal charter of incorporation was granted in 1345, by which time the town's industry and commerce was firmly in the hands of the guilds. It was the time when the two great churches of St John's and St Michael's were constructed, and a city wall three miles long, with 32 towers and 12 gates erected. A poll-tax return for 1377 gives us an estimated population of around 7000, making Coventry the fourth town in England after London, Norwich and Bristol. Coventry was seen as a boom town, attracting an influx of people from surrounding villages in search of work. Immigration was even more pronounced during the Dissolution, when the enclosure of monastic and ecclesiastical estates led to a massive depopulation throughout much of Warwickshire and Northamptonshire; many came to Coventry to find work, or to beg.

The Coventry of the 18th century was still dominated by the wool trade, though by 1765 the manufacture of silk ribbons had become a major local industry and would remain so well into the 19th century. The town was also noted for watchmaking; the Chapelfields would develop into a watchmakers' district of small workshops and skilled craftsmen. In 1768 the Coventry Canal Act was passed. The two principal objectives were to link Coventry to the Grand Trunk Canal and to open up a supply line for cheap coals from the Bedworth coalfield. As there were no locks between Coventry and Atherstone, coal traffic was soon moving; even so, the authorised capital was soon spent, engineer James Brindley had be given the sack, and wrangles with other canal companies meant that the terminus at Fazeley was not reached until 1790.

By 1801 the population stood at 16,000, increasing to 30,700 by 1841 and nearly 41,000 twenty years later. The city did have physical problems in expanding. It was virtually surrounded by common fields known as the Lammas and Michaelmas lands, and this was a direct cause in the development between 1840 and 1860 of the separate township of Hillfields.

The earliest pictures of Coventry in the Frith Collection date from about 1884, though we have a more positive date of 1892, the dawn of the town's second golden age, for the bulk of them. In 1868 the Coventry Machinists' Co won an order to build 300 bicycles on sub-contract for the Paris market. The first bicycles to be made for sale originated from the Paris workshops of coach repairer Pierre Michaux. By 1865 Michaux and his sons had opened a bicycle factory and were capable of producing 400 machines a year. At the time, Coventry Machinists probably considered the sub-contract as just another job, but it was the catalyst for a whole new industry. In 1874 Ariel set up shop in Spon Street; it was the first firm to concentrate solely upon the manufacture of bicycles, and by the mid 1890s there were 80 cycle firms in and around the town. Innovations included tricycles from Humber and Coventry Lever and quadricycles from the likes of Coventry Machinists. The tandem quadricycle roadster from Coventry Machinists could even be converted into a single tricycle by removing either the front or rear wheels. Further advances came in 1896 when the Daimler Motor Syndicate moved into an old cotton mill in the town. Their first engines were not powerful enough to drive a horseless carriage, but were ideal for strapping onto bicycles; thus they played a part in the founding of the motorcycle industry, though neither Daimler nor Daimler-Benz themselves went into motorcycle production. In 1900 local firm Perks & Birch came up with a novel idea for converting the pedal cycle into a motorcycle, by fitting their motor wheel in place of the rear wheel. The Singer Co also adopted the Perks & Birch motor wheel for use in their tricycles.

At the beginning of the 20th century Coventry was being described as 'an ancient city with 69,877 inhab, in 1901, which has grown rapidly since 1875 in consequence of the enormous expansion of the cycle-manufacturing industry, of which it is the headquarters. It possesses also manufacturies of motor-cars, sewing machines, ribbons and watches.' In 1904 the town received a further boost when it was selected by Courtaulds for their main plant. In 1907 there were 332 employees, by 1939 there were 5000, and by 1963 the figure had risen to 7000.

WOLVERHAMPTON, DUDLEY STREET c1900 W285007
Here we see the hustle and bustle of Dudley Street at the beginning of the 20th century. High street chain stores are already in evidence: Freeman, Hardy & Willis, and H Samuel. Hyam & Co, who supplied everything for the gentleman, offered a range of footwear with unusual names: the Eric at 10s 6d a pair, the Edis at 12s 6d, and the Esmond at 14s 6d.

FREEMAN HARDY & WILLIS
COWIN
COWIN
BILLIARDS
ALES

WOLVERHAMPTON, DARLINGTON STREET 1890 W285003
In the days of horse-drawn trams Darlington Street was considered wide enough for a single line only, and here inbound and outbound cars have made use of the passing loop. As can be seen, double-deck cars required a pair of horses to pull them, sometimes three if the going was particularly steep. These cars could carry about 20 passengers in the saloon and 24 on the top deck.

STOBART
TAILOR
CIGAR

WOLVERHAMPTON, QUEEN STREET c1900 W285001
As well as retail outlets and the main post office, there were a number of buildings along Queen Street which dated from the earlier decades of the 19th century, including the Mechanics' Institute and Athenaeum (1835); the Dispensary with its Doric demi-columns (1826); and the County Court, the ground floor of which was built in 1813, the upper storey being added in 1829.

WOLVERHAMPTON, QUEEN SQUARE 1910 W285002
With a DA registration plate, the automobile is from the Wolverhampton area, and appears to be chauffeur-driven. In the years immediately prior to the Great War, a number of British car manufacturers got round the problem of the poor state of most of the country's roads by offering 'colonial' versions of their touring cars. These had greater ground clearance than vehicles manufactured for the domestic market. In 1913 Standard offered a four-wheel drive.

Wolverhampton, Queen Square 1890 W285006

Judging by the number of straw boaters being worn, our photographer picked a sunny day to tramp around Wolverhampton. In the background near to the Cafe Royal can be seen the equestrian statue erected to the memory of Prince Albert.

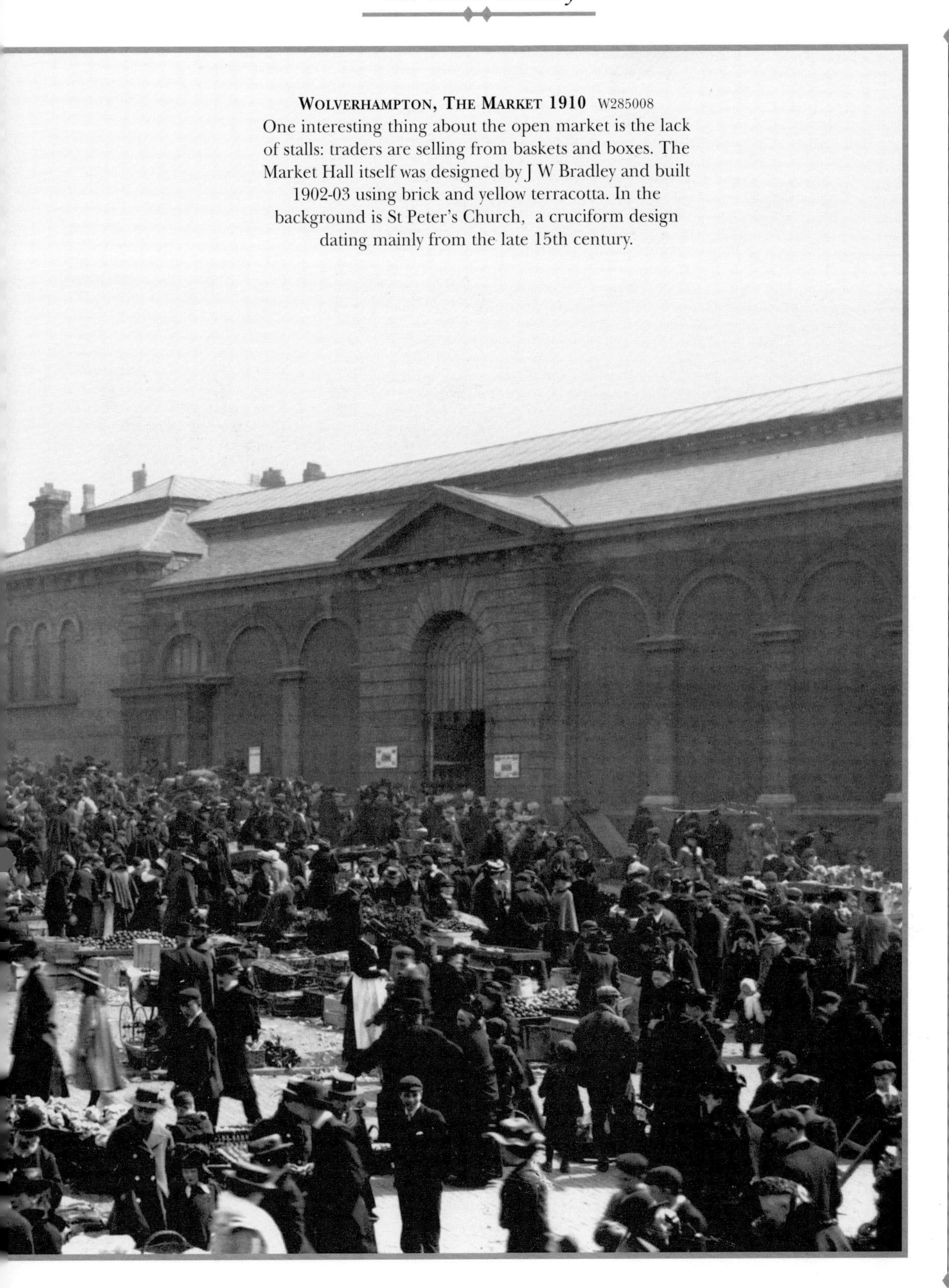

Wolverhampton, The Market 1910 W285008
One interesting thing about the open market is the lack of stalls: traders are selling from baskets and boxes. The Market Hall itself was designed by J W Bradley and built 1902-03 using brick and yellow terracotta. In the background is St Peter's Church, a cruciform design dating mainly from the late 15th century.

WOLVERHAMPTON, VICTORIA STREET 1910 W285005
John Cavit Sons & Co was the place to go for home furnishings, though we cannot quite make out if there is an offer on end of roll carpets, or rolls of linoleum. Linoleum became popular in the late 19th century; it was cheap, hygienic, less slippery than wood or stone flooring, and available in plain colours or patterns.

WOLVERHAMPTON, LICHFIELD STREET 1910 W285004

Of interest here are what at first appear to be tiles laid several feet apart down the centre of the tram tracks. These are in fact the Lorrain stud-collectors from which the Wolverhampton trams picked up their power; as you can see, there are no overhead wires. The tram picked up current by means of a skate fitted underneath, the theory being that the stud-collector was sprung and would only become live when a tram passed over it. Most of the time it worked extremely well, but there are recorded incidents of springs failing and the collectors remaining live, electrocuting pedestrians and horses alike.

PENN, THE OLD CHURCH C1955 P157001

Though now a suburb of Wolverhampton, Penn was one of a number of Staffordshire place-names of Celtic derivation; Walsall is another. The church is dedicated to St Bartholomew. Its tower was encased in brick in 1765.

Tettenhall, The Green c1960 T140006

Tettenhall
The Green c1960
Just two miles from Wolverhampton, Tettenhall retained its two greens despite the Enclosure Commissioners. In AD910 Tettenhall was the scene of one of the most important battles in English history. It was here that Edward the Elder of Wessex defeated the Danes. The battle marked a turning point. From then onwards the English went over to the offensive, Edward's ultimate aim being the total reconquest of the Danelaw. The Anglo-Saxon Chronicle tells us that 'this year, the army of the Danes and the English fought at Totanheale on the eighth of the Ides of August, and the English had the victory'.

Tettenhall
The Clock Tower c1960
West Park was laid out between 1879-81 by R H Vertegans. Interestingly, the park was one of those that managed to hang on to its original gates and railings when others lost theirs to the drive for salvage scrap during the war. The layout of the park is informal.

Tettenhall, The Clock Tower c1960 T140005

GRANTS

Bilston, Street Scene c1960

As at Tipton and Wednesbury, the 30 ft seam of Thick Coal was near the surface at Bilston. Though there is evidence for coal pits at the time of Edward I, Bilston came into its own during the 19th century. In 1827 local mines produced an estimated 317,000 tonnes, and by the mid 1860s output was around 10 million tonnes. The population expanded from 6900 in 1801 to 24,000 in 1861.

BILSTON, ST LEONARD'S PARISH CHURCH 1968 B353002

BILSTON
St Leonard's Parish Church 1968
Though medieval in origin, St Leonard's was completely rebuilt by Francis Goodwin in the mid 1820s: note the long round-arched windows along the side of the building. The interior was remodelled between 1883 and 1893, though it retained its late 17th-century font.

BILSTON
The Greyhound Inn c1960
Located in the High Street, it is thought that the Greyhound Inn could be as early as the mid 15th century. Note that the gables are not in line.

BILSTON, THE GREYHOUND INN c1960 B353005

WALSALL, ST MATTHEW'S CHURCH 1967 W161009

St Matthew's was rebuilt in a pseudo-Gothic style in 1775, with additional work being carried out in 1820. The chancel is built on a slope, and because of the gradient is supported by a vaulted passage under its east end; a similar situation exists at All Saints, Ecclesall, near Sheffield.

WALSALL, PARK STREET 1967 W161018

A hundred years or so before this picture was taken Park Street was already a street of shops. In the 1850s Harry Grove the chemist was the place to go for Grove's tonic tincture which 'will relieve most acute pain instantaneously, arising either from a carious tooth or soreness of the gums'. Harry also marketed Grove's succedaneum, or everlasting enamel for stopping decaying teeth. Other businesses in Harry's day were Barrett's the tailors and general clothiers; the unfortunately named W Rotten (Junior), fish salesman and dealer in game and poultry; George French the auctioneer; and William Gough, saddler, collar and harness maker.

WALSALL, THE BRIDGE 1908 W161001

The Bridge was a busy tram interchange and terminus. After Wolverhampton, Walsall is the largest of the Black Country towns. Between 1801 and 1901 its population rose from 10,000 to 87,000 - and it is considerably higher today at over 184,000. Though famous for its leather goods, Walsall grew up on coal and ironstone mining, iron working, and limestone quarrying.

WEDNESBURY, HIGH STREET c1960 W235012

Originally called Woden's Bury, the town might be the Wodensbeorge mentioned in the Anglo-Saxon Chronicle. If so, then it has a somewhat bloody history. In AD592 the Chronicle relates of a great slaughter in Britain at Wodensbeorge during a pitched battle between the Mercians and the West Saxons. In AD715 there was a return fixture when the armies of Ina, King of Wessex and Ceolred, King of Mercia clashed.

WEDNESBURY, ST PAUL'S CHURCH C1965 W235003

Wednesbury grew rapidly between 1851 and 1861 with the opening of firms like the Old Park Works and Lloyds, Foster & Co. However, during the slump of 1875-1886 the town suffered, with nine out of its eleven iron firms going out of business. There is little of pre-18th-century Wednesbury left save for the parish church.

WEST BROMWICH, OAK HOUSE MUSEUM C1965 W237020

The former home of the Turton family features a half-timbered lantern and tall clustered chimneys. Though the front of the house is half-timbered, the back is Jacobean brick. The building was purchased by Alderman Farley in 1895 and restored for use as the town museum.

West Bromwich
High Street 1963

West Bromwich was one of four Staffordshire county boroughs created in 1889; the others were Hanley, Walsall and Wolverhampton. Between 1801 and 1901 the town's population rose from 5600 to over 65,000 owing to its becoming a centre for iron-making.

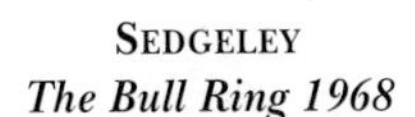

Sedgeley
The Bull Ring 1968

By the late 13th century both coal and ironstone were being mined in the Sedgeley area, and by the end of the 17th century the town was noted for nail-making; Robert Plot in his book 'The Natural History of Staffordshire' (1696), states that nailing kept 2000 men and boys employed in Sedgeley alone.

West Bromwich, High Street 1963 W237016

Sedgeley, The Bull Ring 1968 S336012

DUDLEY, FROM THE CASTLE c1955 D103016
Standing as it does on its limestone hill, Dudley Castle dominates the town. Rebuilt in stone in the early 12th century, Dudley was slighted in 1175 after its owner, Gervase Pagnell, chose the wrong side in a dispute between Henry II and Prince Henry. The castle passed by marriage to the de Somerys; they rebuilt the fortress in stone, including the keep, gatehouse and curtain wall. During the English Civil War, Dudley was the last castle in Staffordshire to be held for the King, surrendering in May 1646. It was again slighted but remained habitable. In 1750 it was reduced to a ruin by fire.

DUDLEY, THE CASTLE GATEWAY 1949 D103004

DUDLEY

The Castle Gateway 1949

Here we see the castle gateway and entrance to the zoo. Opened in 1937 and set within the castle grounds, the zoo, with over 400 species, became one of the best in the country.

DUDLEY

Castle Street and St Edmund's c1955

This view shows Castle Street before its partial redevelopment in the 1960s. The church is St Edmund's, which was rebuilt in brick and stone in the 1720s after apparently being derelict for about eighty years. It was remodelled in the 19th century and is noted for its unusually long chancel.

DUDLEY, CASTLE STREET AND ST EDMUND'S c1955 D103026

DUDLEY, CASTLE STREET 1968 D103192
The developers have struck in Castle Street. Over on the left Sketchley are offering their famous same day cleaning service, and there are deals to be had at Hartley Carpets, but what's a 'chipette' when it's at home? As for The Castle, it was finished in that bleak sixties style that looked shabby before the paint was even dry, while across the road The Angel looks as solid as ever.

BRIERLEY HILL, HIGH STREET c1967 B355017
There is not a shop to let in sight. Mini cars appear to flavour of the month with the drivers of Brierley Hill. When introduced in 1959 the Mini was radical in its design. It was only 10 ft long, ran on 10 inch wheels, and came with front-wheel drive and independent suspension. The battery was in the boot.

BRIERLEY HILL, THE CHURCH c1965 B355007

The brick-built St Michael's is the oldest church in Brierley Hill, and though it dates from 1765 it was restored between 1873 and 1888, and the tower was rebuilt in 1900. Of the town's other churches, St John's and Christ Church, both on the High Street, are from the mid 1840s, and St Mary's Roman Catholic Church dates from the early 1870s.

BRIERLEY HILL, FROM AMBLECOTE ROAD c1965 B355002

High-rise flats are mushrooming up over Brierley Hill in the days when architects and planners were trying their best to get everyone living like battery chickens. The earliest date with any certainty for people living at Brierley is 1619. By the mid-18th century it was an industrial centre, a successful one once the Stourbridge Canal opened for business.

Brierley Hill, The Canal Locks c1965 B355004

The reasoning behind the construction of the Dudley and Stourbridge Canals was for the transportation of coal from pits around Dudley to the glass works at Stourbridge, and for the export of coals and glass to other areas by means of a junction with the Staffordshire & Worcestershire Canal at Stourton. The Main Line of the Stourbridge Canal swung south and then east around Brierley Hill to meet up with the Dudley Canal at Black Delph Locks. The Dudley Canal passed through Round Oak Steel Works and continued on to join up with the Birmingham Canal via Netherton Tunnel.

Stourbridge, High Street 1931 84688

Between 1914 and 1920 there were huge increases in the price of basic foodstuffs, but by the time this picture was taken they were falling to near pre-war levels. Cheese, which had cost 8d a pound in 1914, had risen to 1s 2d by 1920. By 1931 Stourbridge housewives were paying close on 9d a pound. The price of a dozen eggs had risen from 1s 3d in 1914 to a massive 4s 6d by 1920, but had fallen back to 1s 6d.

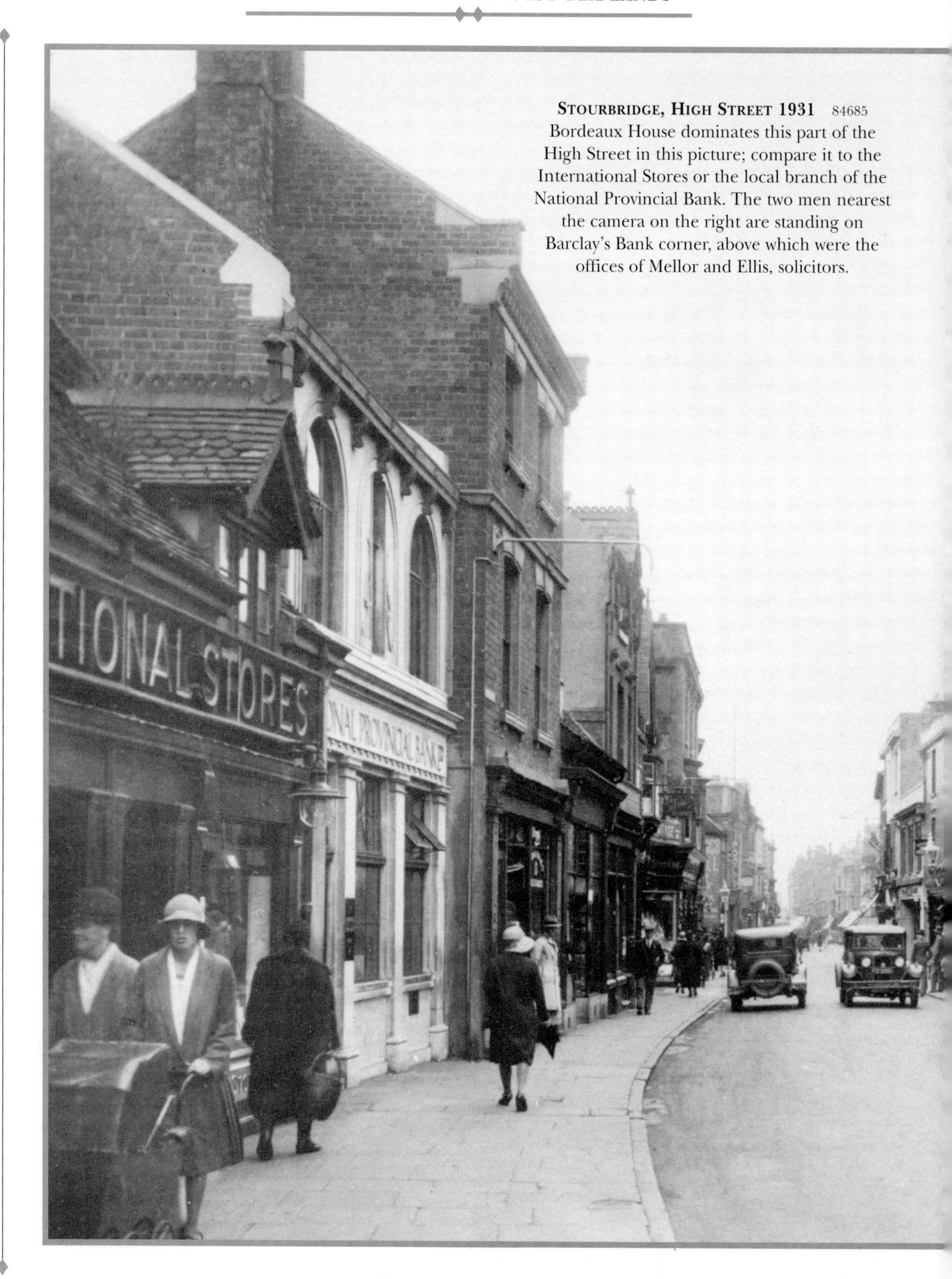

STOURBRIDGE, HIGH STREET 1931 84685
Bordeaux House dominates this part of the High Street in this picture; compare it to the International Stores or the local branch of the National Provincial Bank. The two men nearest the camera on the right are standing on Barclay's Bank corner, above which were the offices of Mellor and Ellis, solicitors.

BORD AUX HOUSE
CORNICE
POLES

STOURBRIDGE, THE TOWN HALL 1931 84683
The design for Stourbridge Town Hall (1887) was by limited, rather than open competition, as were those at Drogheda, Gloucester, Bodmin and Richmond. Most town hall towers were built for show and served no useful purpose. Not so Stourbridge's. It was designed for the storage of documents, and came complete with a strong room. Other councils who insisted on value for money out of their towers were Sheffield and Leeds.

STOURBRIDGE, KING EDWARD VI GRAMMAR SCHOOL c1955 S213004
The school was originally a stipendiary priests' school founded in 1430. Our picture shows the Gothic building designed by Thomas Smith and erected in 1862. Elizabethan-style extensions were added in 1908 and 1911, and New Hall by Webb & Gray was built in 1930-31.

STOURBRIDGE, LOWER HIGH STREET c1960 S213009
This view looks down Lower High Street, where the King Edward VI Grammar School can be seen on the right. In those days it was Fosters for clothes and the Corner Shop for wines, spirits, Butler's Ales, and the dreaded Armadillo sherry.

STOURBRIDGE, THE MITRE INN c1965 S213170
Here we look towards the Mitre Inn at the top of Lower High Street. Since photograph No S213009 was taken the old, and some of them ornate, street lamps have been replaced by concrete, a one-way traffic system has been introduced and there are several new road signs. Still standing, however, is the Market Hall dating from 1827 and its ornate clock.

STOURBRIDGE, THE LIBRARY AND THE WAR MEMORIAL 1931 84684
The Library at the corner of Hagley Road and Church Street was designed by F Woodward and built in 1905. Constructed in red brick and terracotta, it is a happy confusion of Tudor meeting the Baroque.

Stourbridge, St Thomas' Church 1931 84692
In 1931 a number of Stourbridge's places of worship were Victorian, but St Thomas' and the Presbyterian Church, Lower High Street were both Georgian. Built of brick with stone dressings and featuring a partly balustraded parapet, St Thomas' was erected between 1728 and 1736. Additional work was carried out in the 1890s when the apse was added and the tower altered.

Stourbridge, Mary Steven's Park 1931 84698
The ornate fountain was just one of the features of Mary Steven's Park. The grassed areas were interspersed with trees and crossed by winding pathways; there was a lake, paddling pool and children's playground.

Stourbridge, Kidderminster Road 1931 84689
It is hole in the road time again as the lads from Stourbridge gas works prepare to do their stuff. In 1871 W Harrison, secretary of the Birmingham Gas Co, certainly did his stuff; he cooked the books and made off with £18,000. When the company was dissolved, £100 was left in the kitty for Harrison's prosecution in the event of his ever returning to England.

OLD SWINFORD, THE CHURCH 1931 84691

The ancient parish and manor of Old Swinford has in effect disappeared, having been absorbed into Stourbridge, Lye, and Wollescote. The church is dedicated to St Mary; apart from the tower and spire, it was entirely rebuilt in the 1840s, with a new chancel being added in 1898. The tower with its diagonal niche buttresses is late 14th-century.

Old Swinford
The Hospital c1965

Situated to the north of the old village along the Hagley road, the hospital was founded in 1670 by Thomas Foley as almshouses for sixty boys. The hospital is three-storey, the top one being in the gables; a distinctive feature is the two lines each of eight chimneys. The cupola was a later addition.

Kingswinfor
St Mary's Church c1960

Though St Mary's has a Norman tympanum over the south doorway, the date of the present structure is uncertain; Pevsner thought it was either Georgian or early Victorian. On the edge of the Black Country, the town was once known as Swinford and became Kingswinford when a royal manor was established.

Old Swinford, The Hospital c1965 O51005

Kingswinford, St Mary's Church c1960 K84013

KINGSWINFORD, THE SHOPPING CENTRE c1965 K84009
Is the Millennium Dome at Greenwich based on Kingswinford shopping centre? Perhaps we should be told! This picture was taken in the days when we had real money and no one had heard of new pence. In 1967 a dozen eggs cost 4s 1d; 2lb of sugar 1s 9d; potatoes were 5d a pound; a pint of milk 10d; streaky bacon 3s 6d a pound; and for the well off, sirloin was 6s 10d a pound.

CASTLE BROMWICH, THE VILLAGE c1965 C281006
Castle Bromwich, just five miles north-east of the city, was incorporated into Birmingham in 1931. In those days it was still very much a village. To the north of the church were the remains of a motte, the village was served by the early Georgian church of St Mary and St Margaret, and nearby was Castle Bromwich Hall.

CASTLE BROMWICH, CHESTER ROAD c1965 C281001

The development of Castle Bromwich really got under way in the 1930s with the Hodgehill Common housing estate. After the second world war, in which Castle Bromwich played a major part with its Spitfire factory, there were further housing developments at Bucklands End and the Firs. About the time this picture was taken, plans by Sheppard Fidler had been accepted for a 461-acre development to include sixteen-storey tower blocks, two shopping centres, schools, community buildings and parks.

ASTON, ASTON HALL PARK AND THE CHURCH 1896 37299

ASTON

Aston Hall Park and the Church 1896

The parish church of St Peter and St Paul is the only church within city limits to be mentioned in the Domesday Book. The west tower of four stages and the spire date from the 15th century, though the latter was partially rebuilt in 1776-77. The church itself was extensively remodelled in 1879-90, and further work was done in 1908 when the south aisle and porch were rebuilt.

ASTON

Aston Hall 1896

Begun in 1618 for Sir Thomas Holte, Aston was not completed until 1635. This picture shows the east front; it comprises a main block of seven bays topped by a clock tower and two-stage cupola, and two projecting wings each with a square turret. During the English Civil War, Aston was held for the King by Sir Thomas. It is still possible to see the damage caused by Parliamentarian artillery.

ASTON, ASTON HALL 1896 37295

Aston, Aston Hall, Entrance Hall 1896 37298

The entrance hall marks a change from those built during the Tudor period; this one is built for show rather than for use as a room. The decoration is outstanding, though the marble fireplace and animal frieze are believed to be early 19th-century. On the left can be seen two of the three archways, and between them is some of the oak panelling that rises to the height of the archway cornices.

Handsworth, The Church 1896 37304

On the west side of Aston, Handsworth is famous as the location of the Soho Works where Matthew Boulton and James Watt built their steam pumping engines. Watt invented the condensing steam engine in 1765 and the double-acting engine in 1782. The Soho Works opened in 1775. Both Boulton and Watt are buried in St Mary's Church, Handsworth.

VICTORIA
CAFE

BIRMINGHAM, PARADISE STREET 1896 37274
Designed by Charles Barry, the Birmingham and Midland Institute opened in 1856, the foundation stone having been laid by Prince Albert in November 1855. The institute, which offered a range of evening classes for workers, and was famed for its penny lectures, was one of the earlier projects linked with a major redevelopment of the town centre that began in the 1850s and continued through to the 1870s.

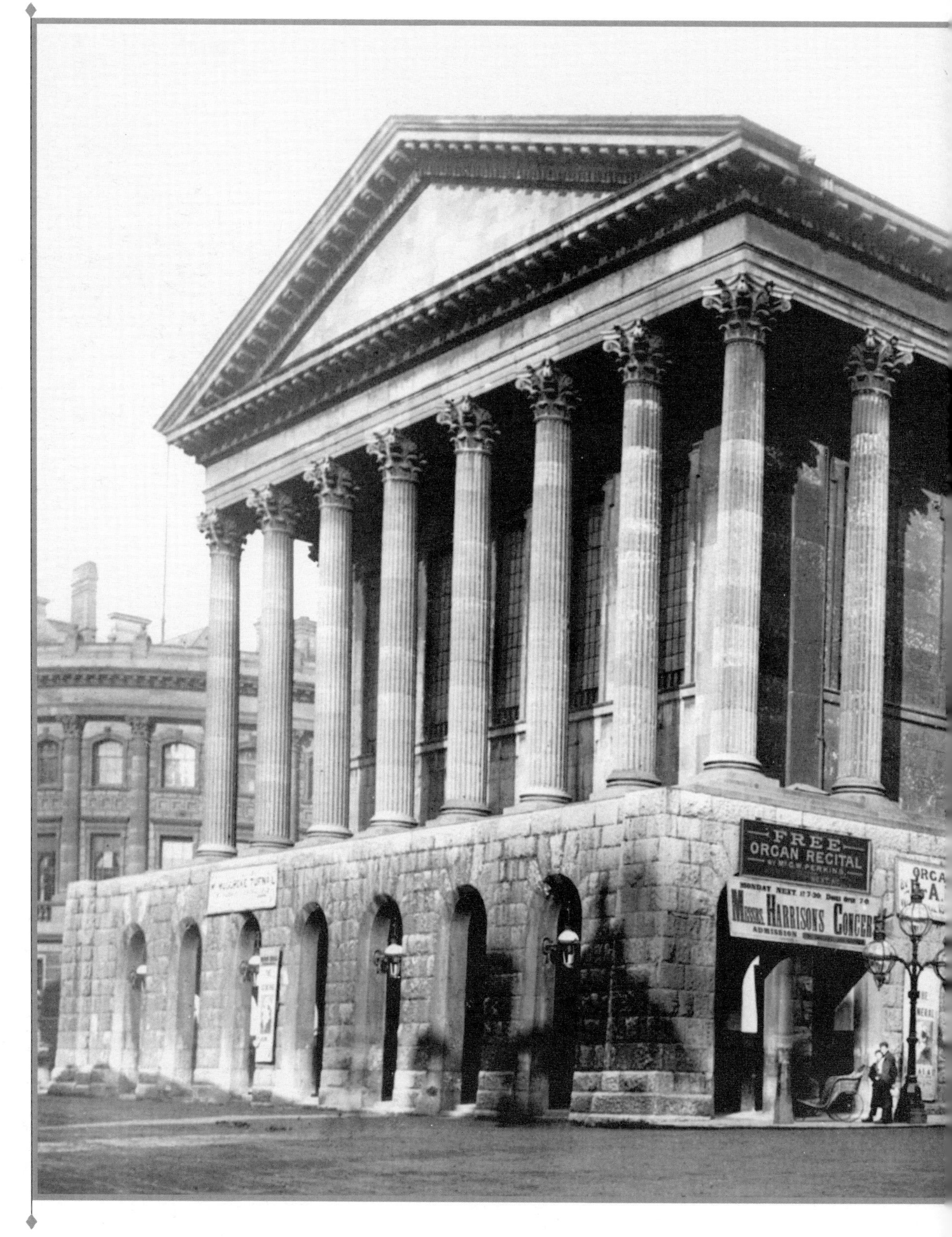
FREE
ORGAN RECITAL
HARRISONS CONCER

BIRMINGHAM, THE TOWN HALL 1896 37275
The competition to design a new town hall was won by J A Hansom and E Welsh; their outline plans were preferred to those submitted by leading architects such as Charles Barry and Thomas Rickman. Work began in 1832, but the project ran into problems owing to a serious underestimate by the builders, who eventually went bankrupt. As the architects had agreed to underwrite the builders, they too were declared bankrupt. Work continued slowly; it was not until 1850 that the building was ready for occupation.

BIRMINGHAM, THE ART GALLERY 1896 37279
Opened in 1885, the Art Gallery and Museum was designed by Yeoville Thomason, who had also designed the adjoining Council House. Much of the money for the gallery came from wealthy glass manufacturer Thomas Osler, whose firm made the famous glass fountain centrepiece for the Great Exhibition at the Crystal Palace. The clock tower is known as Big Brum.

BIRMINGHAM, THE COUNCIL HOUSE 1896 37277
Ann Street and Colmore Row were demolished to make way for the Council House. The first meeting in the council chamber took place on 9th July 1878. Apparently, councillors could not decide what to call their new home, and finished up having to vote on it. Some favoured Municipal Buildings, others were keen on Guildhall, and others wanted Council House; Council House won by 34 votes to 26.

BIRMINGHAM, CHRIST CHURCH 1896 37276

Christ Church, on the corner of Colmore Row and New Street, had a very short career as churches go. The foundation stone was laid in July 1805 by the Earl of Dartmouth on behalf of George III, and when it opened Christ Church was the first church in Birmingham to have free seating, though the sexes were segregated lest passions be aroused. If you look to the right of the church to the corner of New Street you will see an awning. The shops here included Moore's Oyster Rooms, where a dozen of the best would set you back just a few pence. The demolition of Christ Church began in January 1899.

BIRMINGHAM, COLMORE ROW 1896 37272
This view of Colmore Row looks east towards Snow Hill station. The area was redeveloped from 1866; before that it had been a huddle of workshops, shops and dilapidated houses. Demolition of the old properties began after the expiry of their leases.

BIRMINGHAM, NEW STREET 1896 37270

By the end of the 19th century, New Street was both the principal business street in the town and the best for shopping and entertainment. This view is from Paradise Street. On the left just off camera is Christ Church, and over to the right is the Post Office. Known as New Street since the 15th century, the oldest building extant in 1896 was probably No 29, a silversmith and jewellers, that had a rainwater head dated 1687. No 29 was demolished in 1902-03.

BIRMINGHAM, NEW STREET 1890 B100001

This view looks towards the Town Hall. It cost one penny to travel the length of New Street by horse-drawn omnibus, while a Hansom cab cost somewhat more. Cab fares were regulated by the council: a Hansom cost one shilling for the first mile, each additional half-mile costing 4d. They could also be hired by the hour at 2s 6d for the first hour and 6d for each additional quarter hour. The Hansom was designed by J A Hansom, the architect of the Town Hall.

BIRMINGHAM, NEW STREET 1896 37271
New Street was the scene of many events. Large crowds gathered along it for the laying of the foundation stone of the Masonic Hall. In July 1891 windows and balconies were packed to capacity for the visit of the Prince and Princess of Wales, who had come to Birmingham to open the Victoria Law Courts.

BIRMINGHAM, THE GRAMMAR SCHOOL C1890 B100301

In the early 15th century the Guild of the Holy Cross built a hall in New Street; in those days it was on the edge of the township. When the guild was suppressed during the Dissolution, sufficient property was retained to maintain a grammar school, which was founded in 1552. This picture shows the 19th-century New Street premises of the Edward VI school designed in the Tudor style by Charles Barry.

BIRMINGHAM, THE GRAND HOTEL 1896 B100005

Designed by J A Chatwin, the Grand Hotel, Colmore Row, was completed in 1875 and remodelled in 1891. Note the French pavilion-style roofs, a popular design feature of many Victorian hotels. Rooms at the Grand were slightly more expensive than other leading hotels, though prices for meals were on a par with those at the Queen's and the Midland.

Birmingham
St Philip's Church 1896

St Philip's was architect Thomas Archer's first big commission; its grand baroque style was inspired by his wanderings around Europe. The main body of the church was built in 1715, with the tower being added in 1725. The exterior was refaced between 1864-69 and the chancel extended in 1883-84. St Philip's was raised to cathedral status in 1905 with the creation of the diocese of Birmingham.

Birmingham, St Philip's Church 1896 37291

Birmingham
Corporation Street 1896

Described in 1890 as a 'handsome modern thoroughfare', Corporation Street was the result of a massive redevelopment of 93 acres of slums. Councillor Ward said that the 'rubbish and dilapidation of whole quarters have reminded me of Strasbourg which I saw soon after the bombardment'. The area was notorious, wells were contaminated with raw sewage, and the death rate was 3.2 per cent above the national average.

Birmingham, Corporation Street 1896 37269

BIRMINGHAM, CORPORATION STREET 1890 B100002
To the Victorians the most important buildings along Corporation Street were the Victoria Law Courts, the County Court, and the Grand Theatre, but not necessarily in that order. This was also the place in which to eat out. There was the Arcadian at 18 North West Arcade; a branch of Pattisons; then there was Fletchers, and the Stork and Central Hotels. Vegetarians, however, probably had to make their way to Gardes at 25 Paradise Street.

Birmingham, Cannon Hill Park 1896 37302
Cannon Hill Fields were presented to the town in 1873 by Louisa Anne Ryland, and were developed to become Birmingham's fourth park. By 1914 further parks had opened including Highgate, Summerfield, Small Heath, Handsworth, and Queen's Park, Harborne.

Edgbaston, The Church 1896 37305
There is a tradition that a church was founded at Edgbaston in AD775. During the Civil War the local church was all but destroyed by Parliamentarian troops. It appears that a collection was organised to pay for repairs. There exists an entry in the register of St Sepulchre's Church, Northampton for 1657 which states 'seven shillings and sixpence received towards the repairs of the church at Edge Barston, in the county of Warwick'.

EDGBASTON, HAGLEY ROAD 1949 E85002

BOURNVILLE, MARY VALE ROAD 1949 B354050

EDGBASTON
Hagley Road 1949

Edgbaston is the most famous of all Birmingham's suburbs. It was the home of the Chamberlain family, who had an impact on both the development of Birmingham and the history of Britain; the headquarters of Warwickshire County Cricket Club; and the site of the Botanical Gardens. In 1949 the shops along Hagley Road were all taken. Booksellers and stationers T W Atkinson even operated a library from which books could be loaned at 2d a time.

BOURNVILLE,
Mary Vale Road 1949

Situated 4.5 miles south of Birmingham, Bournville was chosen by George Cadbury in 1879 as the site for his new factory and for a model village for his workers. Cadbury was one of the first employers to grasp the importance of the relationship between environment and workplace. Initially 143 homes were built, which were sold at cost price. A 999 year leasing arrangement ensured that gardens and open areas could not be built on.

Bournville, The Carillion c1960 B354104
The Junior Schools, Linden Road were built in 1902-05, a mixture of Tudor Revival and Art Nouveau. The brick tower on the south-east end was erected in 1934 to house one of only four carillons (48 bells) in the country.

KING'S NORTON, THE VILLAGE GREEN c1955 K83008
King's Norton is less than two miles from Bournville, and though urban sprawl between the wars linked it to Birmingham, the old village still retains much of its rural character. The village was a part of Worcestershire until 1911, when it was absorbed into Birmingham.

KING'S NORTON, THE OLD SARACEN'S HEAD 1949 K83007
The village church, dedicated to St Nicholas, is Norman in origin and was partially rebuilt during the 13th century. Within a few decades the church was extended; the west tower with its octagonal spire is 15th-century. The clerestory was added in the 17th century and the north aisle remodelled in the 1870s.

KING'S NORTON, OLD SARACEN'S HEAD INN c1955 K83004

The old inn dates from the late 15th century and comprises three bays with two wings projecting behind either side of a courtyard. The north wing, which is jettied on a moulded wood bressumer, remains half-timbered; the south wing was rebuilt in the 19th century to house the parish hall.

KING'S NORTON, OLD KING EDWARD'S GRAMMAR SCHOOL c1955 K83011

Situated on the north side of the churchyard, this was once the priest's house. The lower floor, which is brick with stone quoins, appears to have been underbuilt in the late 16th century when the porch was added. The external staircase is a somewhat late arrival, being added in 1910.

NORTHFIELD, THE PARISH CHURCH AND GREAT STONE INN c1955 N203003

The parish church of St Laurence is originally 12th-century with a 13th-century chancel. The south aisle was replaced in the late 13th century; the north aisle was only added in 1900, though it was built in a 14th-century style. On the right is the pound, or village lock-up, built of sandstone.

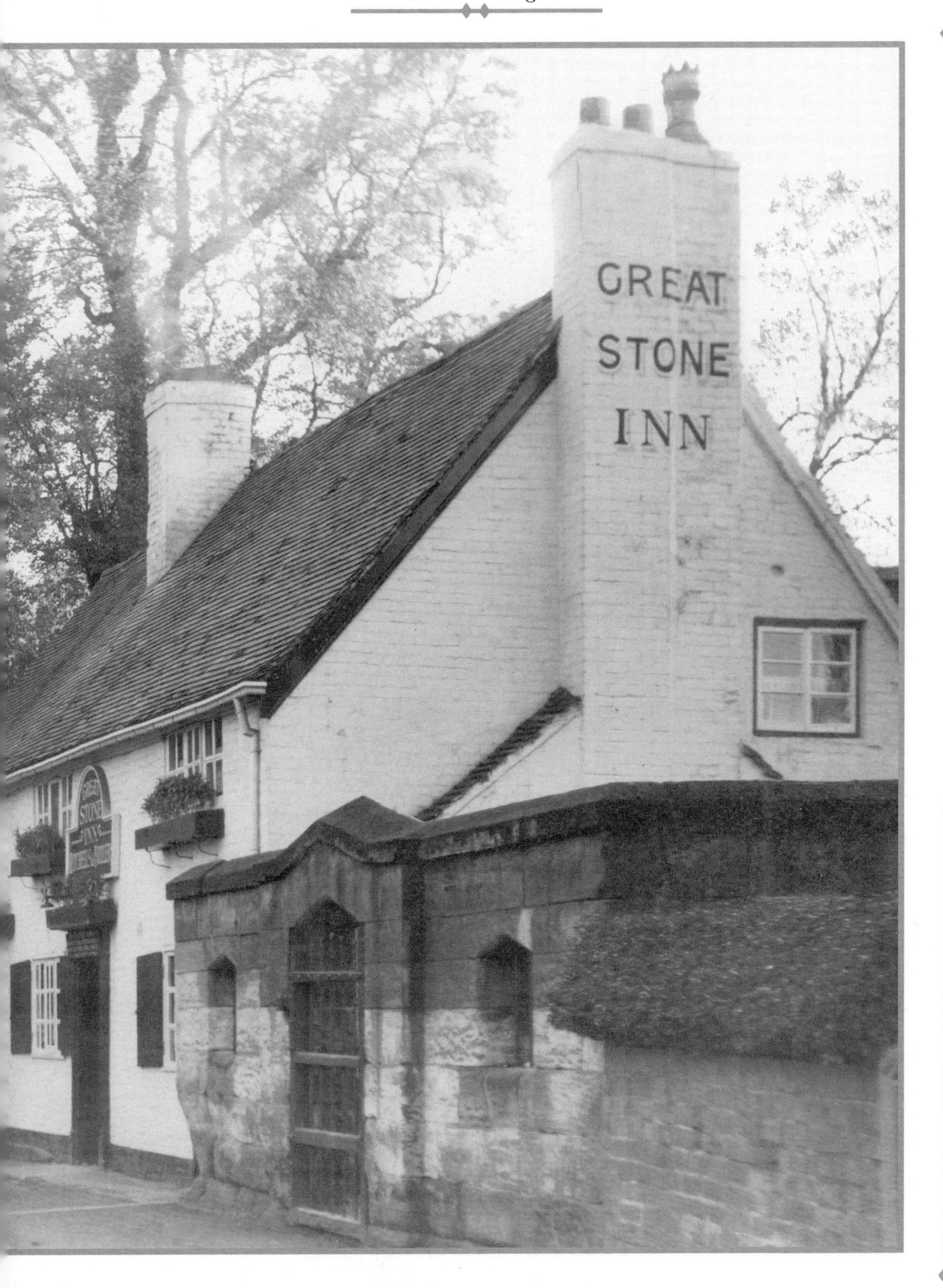
GREAT
STONE
INN

NORTHFIELD, THE BLACK HORSE c1955 N203007

The Great Stone Inn is one of Northfield's older drinking establishments, as is the Old Bell House, Bell Hill. Despite its looks, the Black Horse, Bristol Road, is in fact an excellent mock-Tudor building designed by C E Bateman and built in 1929.

NORTHFIELD, THE ROYAL CRIPPLES HOSPITAL c1955 N203002

The hospital was opened by the Prince of Wales in November 1927, and was also visited by the Duke and Duchess of York in November 1929 when they came to Birmingham to inaugurate Hams Hall Power Station and open Kingston Hill Recreation Ground.

Northfield, Bell Road c1955 N203001

Bell Road is an echo of Northfield's agricultural past. The population grew by over 200 per cent between 1881 and 1891, nearly all of it overflow from Birmingham; but modern Northfield owes much to the opening of the Austin works at Longbridge.

Northfield, Bristol Road South c1955 N203005

It was in February 1909 that proposals were made under the Greater Birmingham Plan to annex Aston Manor, Erdington, Handworth, King's Norton, Northfield and Yardley. The Urban District of King's Norton and Northfield had a population in excess of 78,000 and covered 22,000 acres. The plans would give Birmingham a population of 850,000, making it the second city in England.

ACOCK'S GREEN, YARDLEY ROAD c1965 A136014
Until the 1830s Acock's Green was a small agricultural village. Development really began in 1839 when the old estate, comprising about 150 acres, was given over to building.

ACOCK'S GREEN, YARDLEY ROAD c1965 A136012

YARDLEY, THE UNDERPASS c1965 Y18012

ACOCK'S GREEN
Yardley Road c1965

Both Acock's Green and Olton were once residential areas favoured by the wealthier inhabitants of Birmingham, but they became progressively industrialized as factories opened along the route of the railway. The Birmingham Mail in November 1903 reported that Acock's Green's genteeler residents were moving further out: 'Like the Arab, they are folding their tents and stealing away in the direction of Knowle and Solihull, where the octopus tentacles of expanding Birmingham are as yet in the distance'.

YARDLEY
The Underpass c1965

Situated to the east of Acock's Green, and four miles from the city centre, Yardley is one of the parishes absorbed by Birmingham in 1911. It is crossed by main roads to Warwick, Stratford and Coventry, and our picture harks back to those cone-free days of yester-year.

YARDLEY, BLAKESLEY HALL c1965 Y18016
The half-timbered manor house of Blakesley Hall dates from 1575. Yardley is an ancient manor and parish covering 11.5 square miles, and was once a part of Worcestershire. With the extension of the tramway from Small Heath to the Swan Hotel it became a popular residential suburb for those businessmen wishing to live in more rural surroundings. In 1900 the parish was still predominantly agricultural.

HARBORNE, ST PETER'S CHURCH c1965 H365032
Of the ancient medieval parish church little remains. The red sandstone tower dates from the 15th century, and may itself have been a rebuild on the base of an earlier structure. The remainder dates from 1867 when the church was rebuilt at a cost of £3500.

JOHNSONS
"THE"
YERS
THE DYERS
YERS JOHNSONS' CLEANERS
Davenports

Harborne, High Street c1955 H365011
The High Street sports a branch of F W Woolworth, and the local branch of the National Provincial Bank is housed in half-timbered style premises. The church of St John Baptist was designed by none other than Yeoville Thomason, architect of Birmingham Council House. Thomason was also responsible for rebuilding St Peter's, Harborne.

HARBORNE, PRINCES CORNER C1965 H365023

HARBORNE, THE CHAPEL, BIRMINGHAM BLUE COAT SCHOOL C1955 H365002

HARBORNE
Princes Corner c1965

The pub on the corner was always a handy place for a quick lunchtime pint, and even in 1965 for a pie. Of Harborne's pubs, the Bell, Old Church Street has survived for three hundred years; its bar is in the passageway. The Junction, High Street has one very big room, an island bar, and some fixtures and fittings supplied by the Bass Museum.

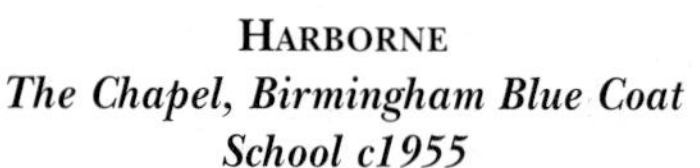

HARBORNE
The Chapel, Birmingham Blue Coat School c1955

The original Birmingham Blue Coat School was founded in 1724 and was housed in premises on the east side of St Philip's churchyard. The school moved to Harborne in the 1930s.

HARBORNE, THE BLUE COAT SCHOOL c1965 H365003

The Blue Coat School, Somerset Road, was built in 1930, having been designed by J F Bell and H W Simister. As can be seen, the main entrance is designed in the 18th-century style. The statues in the niches are of a boy and a girl wearing school uniform, and are copies of original figures by Samuel and Edward Grubb.

HARBORNE, GROVE PARK c1965 H365034

Whether Harborne is famous for being a good place to catch newts and minnows is not recorded, but it was famous as a place for growing gooseberries; the annual dinner of the Gooseberry Growers' Society was first held in Harborne in 1815. In the second half of the 19th century Harborne was something of a go-ahead place. In 1865 it became a tradition to treat the aged poor to Christmas dinner. In the 1880s it opened its own Institute and Masonic Hall, and a condition of it joining Birmingham was that it got its own free library. Harborne was added to Birmingham in 1891, along with Saltley and Balsall Heath, and Edgbaston was amalgamated with Harborne to form a new ward.

Rednal, The Steps, Licky Hills c1960 R250071

Much of the area around Rednal would have been built on in the 1880s, had it not been for the intervention of the Birmingham Association for the Preservation of Open Spaces. They managed to save 32 acres of countryside from the grasping paws of developers; the land was later acquired by Birmingham Corporation. Edward and George Cadbury provided additional funds for the outright purchase of the adjoining Bilberry Hill.

Coventry, The Three Spires c1890 C169002
A classic view of the three spires. The spires are those of St Michael's (295 ft), Holy Trinity (237 ft), and the octagonal steeple (230 ft) of Christ Church. Christ Church is a remnant of the Grey Friar's monastery demolished in 1539. Both Christ Church and St Michael's were bombed during the second world war.

Coventry, St John's Hospital 1892 30919
Founded in the 12th century, the hospital of St John Baptist offered temporary relief to poor wayfarers and relief to the sick and poor of the city. St John's benefited from a number of bequests, including a weekly load of wood; this was negotiated by Roger de Montalt, Earl of Chester, when he sold off his lordship rights in the Earl's Half to the Prior. St John's was disbanded during the Reformation, and the building later used for a free school.

COVENTRY, ST JOHN'S CHURCH c1884 17127
Built of red sandstone, St John's has links with Queen Isabella (1292-1358) and the Guild of St John Baptist (founded 1342). It was restored by Sir G G Scott in 1877, though the corbelled turrets on the tower are early 19th-century additions.

COVENTRY, HIGH STREET AND BROADGATE c1955 C169003
By 1941 planning was well under way to rebuild the shattered heart of Coventry. The Broadgate shopping precinct, a series of squares with shops on two levels, was an excellent idea, even if the finished product was dull. In the picture we have two buildings from the 1930s: Lloyd's Bank (1932) with its giant arch, and the National Provincial Bank with its neo-classical portico.

COVENTRY, BISHOP STREET 1892 30914
Sandwiched between St Nicholas Street and the old market place at Cross Cheaping, Bishop Street was one of Coventry's main shopping thoroughfares. As can be seen, the street was served by horse-drawn trams. In 1895 Coventry became one of the early converts to electric street tramways; the system operated until November 1940, when it suffered heavy damage during the blitz.

Coventry, Butcher Row 1892 C169001

Coventry has undergone massive redevelopment since the end of the second world war, not only with projects such as the Broadgate shopping precinct, but an American-inspired partly-elevated ring-road that surrounds the old city centre. Few streets still follow their original medieval plans, though not all have been lost since 1945. Butcher Row went long ago.

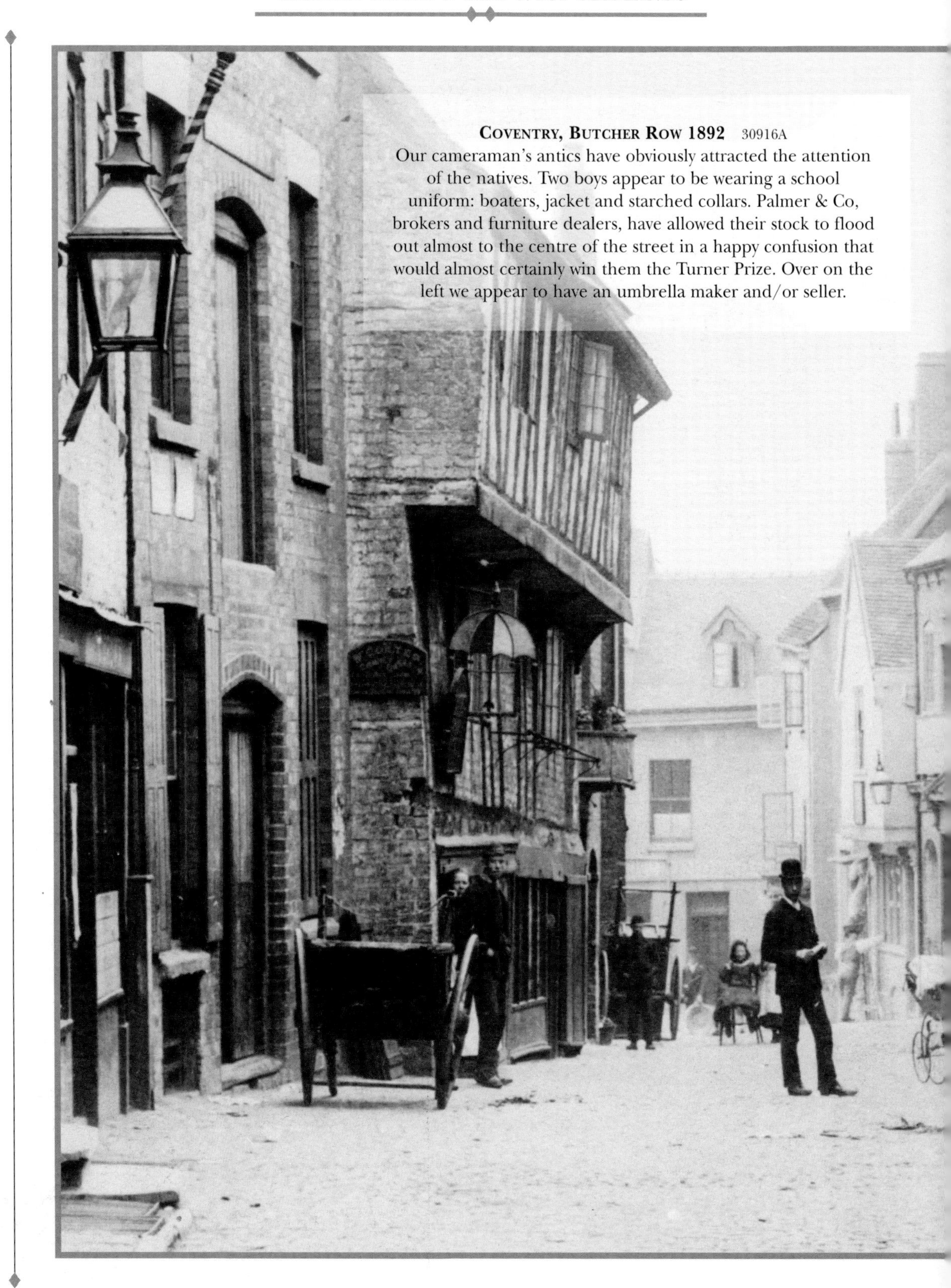

COVENTRY, BUTCHER ROW 1892 30916A
Our cameraman's antics have obviously attracted the attention of the natives. Two boys appear to be wearing a school uniform: boaters, jacket and starched collars. Palmer & Co, brokers and furniture dealers, have allowed their stock to flood out almost to the centre of the street in a happy confusion that would almost certainly win them the Turner Prize. Over on the left we appear to have an umbrella maker and/or seller.

BROKERS
DEALERS.

COVENTRY, HOLY TRINITY CHURCH 1892 30927

The parish church in the Prior's Half, Holy Trinity was already a large church in the late 13th century. The present structure dates from c1360, though the chancel was begun in 1391 and the Marler Chapel was added in 1537. Holy Trinity has been restored on a number of occasions; the tower and spire were rebuilt 1665-68, the east end was rebuilt in 1786, and the west end in 1826.

COVENTRY, THE BLUE COAT SCHOOL AND PRIORY RUINS c1890 C169301
The Benedictine Priory, founded in 1043, grew to become one of the wealthiest in the midlands, and the sheer bulk of its buildings must have made an imposing sight on the Coventry skyline. The complex included a church about 400 ft long; a cloister on the north side; the west front was supported by towers or turrets; and there were two chapels radiating off from the chancel. The base of one of the towers was incorporated into the north wall of the Blue Coat School.

COVENTRY, HOLY TRINITY CHURCH 1892 30928

Holy Trinity, with its superb timbered ceilings, 15th-century stone pulpit, brass eagle lectern, and octagonal font with panelled stem, is one of just a handful of buildings that survive from Coventry's medieval past. The interior underwent restoration in the 1850s.

COVENTRY, ST MICHAEL'S CHURCH c1884 17124

This was the parish church in the Earl's Half; with a floor area of 24,000 sq ft, St Michael's was one of the most impressive and possibly the largest parish church in England. St Michael's housed six chapels belonging to the town's dyers, cappers, mercers, smiths, girdlers, and drapers.

COVENTRY, ST MICHAEL'S CHURCH 1892 30922

The church dates from the late 13th to the early 16th centuries, with work on the steeple beginning in the 1370s. Note how the bell-openings are flanked by statues, and the spire sits on an octagonal storey supported by slim flying buttresses. From this picture we get some idea of just how wide the church is: the nave is wider than the steeple is high.

COVENTRY, ST MICHAEL'S CHURCH 1892 30925

The 14th century has often been described as a golden age for Coventry. It was the period when its guilds were founded, the charter of incorporation granted, and the city walls constructed. A poll-tax return for 1377 gives a population of 7000, making Coventry the fourth largest city in medieval England after London, Bristol and Norwich.

COVENTRY, THE CATHEDRAL c1965 C169076

When Basil Spence designed the new cathedral, he incorporated the ruins of St Michael's into the scheme of things: the old church in effect became the new cathedral's vestibule. Spence's design was attacked by traditionalists for being too modern; others saw it as a statement of Coventry's renewal following the blitz. How Spence came up with the design is interesting. He said that it was whilst under the influence of an anaesthetic for toothache that he saw zigzagging walls and an altar ablaze with light. His use of curves helped to disguise the fact that the nave of the new building was only 270 ft long and 80 ft wide: quite small in cathedral terms. By the entrance is Epstein's St Michael and Lucifer, one of his last works.

Coventry, St Mary's Hall 1892 30929

Built 1340-42 as the hall of the Merchant Guild, St Mary's was enlarged in around 1400 for the Trinity Guild. The Great Hall is famed for an early 16th-century tapestry of Flemish origin, which is thought to commemorate the visit of Henry VII and Elizabeth of York.

COVENTRY, ST MARY'S HALL 1892 30930

Here we see the courtyard of St Mary's Hall. In 1892 the Hall also featured Caesar's Tower, a 13th-century structure, part of which is thought to have belonged to Coventry Castle. The tower was the only part of the Hall to be badly damaged during the second world war, though it as since been reconstructed.

COVENTRY
The Stocks, St Mary's Hall c1890

The stocks, along with the pillory and the whipping post, were instruments of punishment at one time in use throughout England. The stocks were usually positioned on a main thoroughfare, or better still in the market place; convicted wrongdoers were secured in them by either their legs or arms. Punishment might well involve several sessions in the stocks on consecutive market days. The wrongdoer, wearing a notice around his or her neck which gave details of the offence, would be left for an hour or so to face public ridicule and humiliation.

COVENTRY
Ford's Hospital 1892

In 1509 William Ford, a merchant, founded and endowed the Greyfriar's Hospital, a half-timbered almshouse for five poor men and their wives. It was just one of a number of generous donations made to the city during the 16th century; others included Bond's (Bablake) Hospital for poor men founded in 1506, and Bablake Boys' Hospital in 1560.

COVENTRY, THE STOCKS, ST MARY'S HALL c1890 C169302

COVENTRY, FORD'S HOSPITAL 1892 30918

COVENTRY, FORD'S HOSPITAL 1892 30917
Ford's Hospital was hit during the blitz of 14 November 1940. The gable nearest our cameraman was destroyed, and part of the front of the upper storey blown out. The building was restored in 1953; a great effort was made to use as much as was salvageable from the original.

WILLENHALL, MARKET PLACE c1965 W238010
The ornate fountain and clock tower forms the centrepiece of the Market Place, but it looks as though Willenhall will soon have another attraction, the Zorba Grill - no doubt inspired by the film starring Anthony Quinn.

CHASEWATER c1965 C280006
Once a canal feeder, Chasewater was developed for recreational purposes in the late 1950s offering sailing and boating. In 1967 it was the venue for the world's first 24-hour international powerboat race. Since 1966 Chasewater has been the home of the Chasewater Light Railway Co, whose line runs alongside the reservoir.

CHASEWATER, HOVERCRAFT c1965 C280005
Invented by Christopher Cockerell, the Hovercraft is propelled on a cushion of air and can travel with ease over land, swamp, marshy ground or water. When this picture was taken there were very few privately-built Hovercraft around, so this one was bound to draw attention to itself.

SUTTON COLDFIELD, SUTTON PARK c1960 S339039
Sutton Park was one of the largest in Warwickshire, over 2000 acres of woodlands and lakes. The park made the town something of a tourist attraction. During Whit-week 1882 the town had over 19,000 visitors; in 1883 it had 11,300; and in 1884 it had 17,400.

Sutton Coldfield, High Street c1965 S339055

An old market town on the road to Lichfield only seven miles from Birmingham, Sutton Coldfield hung on to its independence until annexed by its large neighbour in 1974. Though an important town in the Middle Ages, Sutton Coldfield's development took off in the 16th century thanks to John Veysey. A local man, John was eventually appointed Bishop of Exeter, and it was he who founded the school, paved the streets, and built the Moot Hall and other places. It was at Sutton Coldfield that Charles I reviewed his troops in October 1642 prior to the battle of Edge Hill.

NO ENTRY
ONE WAY STREET

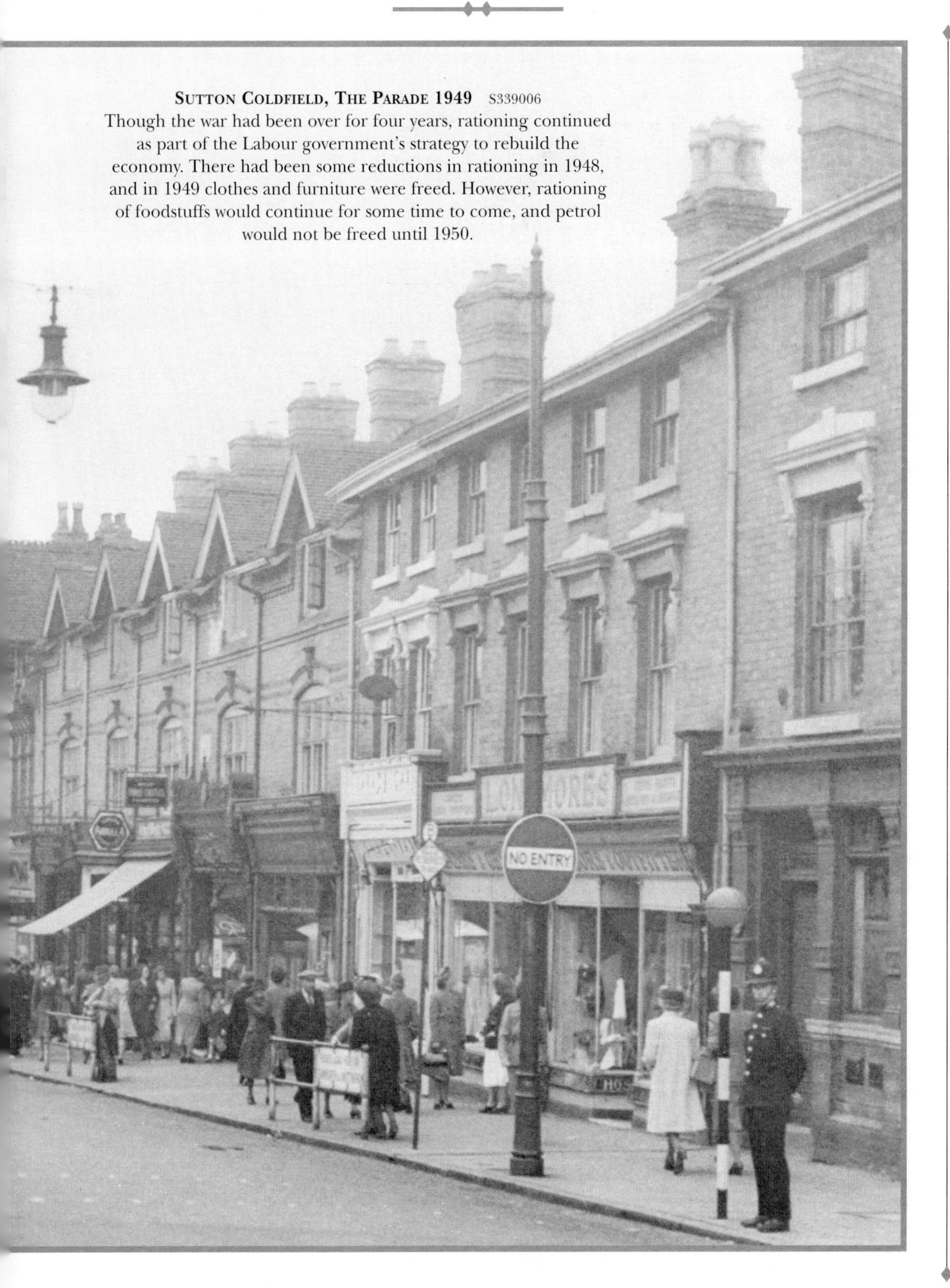

SUTTON COLDFIELD, THE PARADE 1949 S339006
Though the war had been over for four years, rationing continued as part of the Labour government's strategy to rebuild the economy. There had been some reductions in rationing in 1948, and in 1949 clothes and furniture were freed. However, rationing of foodstuffs would continue for some time to come, and petrol would not be freed until 1950.

SUTTON COLDFIELD, THE PARADE c1949 S339003

Bearing in mind that rationing was still in force on some foodstuffs in 1949, price increases on basic items since the early 1930s varied wildly. For instance, potatoes were 1d a pound in 1933 and were the same in 1949, and over the same period the cost of a pound of streaky bacon had risen by just 1d to 1s 6d. However, the price of a pint of milk had rocketed from 1d in 1933 to 5d, and a 3lb bag of flour had gone up from 5d to 11d.

SOLIHULL, HIGH STREET 1968 S257084

In 1885 Solihull was described as a 'very pleasant village, but a few miles distant'. Even so, the population then was about 6000. The town's development received a boost in 1945 when Rover announced their intention to abandon their Coventry plant and concentrate production at their former shadow factory at Solihull.

Solihull, Mell Square c1965 S257022
As with many other towns, the centre of Solihull was redeveloped in the 1960s. Among the projects was a new civic centre designed by H Weedon & Partners, and the demolition of Drury Lane for a pedestrian shopping precinct.

Solihull, Malvern Hall School c1965 S257049
Just to the south of Solihull, Malvern Hall was built of stone in the early 18th century; the original building was probably of seven bays with a three-bay centre. The Hall survived to become a school.

Shirley, The Village 1890 27845
Situated within the parish of Solihull, Shirley was still rural enough in the 1880s and 90s to become a popular destination for those who enjoyed a Sunday drive.

Shirley, Stratford Road c1955 S337001
Shirley became a location for a number of industries, and two buildings in particular stand out. The first, in Cranmore Boulevard, is an office range built in 1954-56 for Carrs and designed by Erno Goldfinger. The second, designed by Clifford Tee & Gale and built in 1963-65, is the research labs of Joseph Lucas Ltd on Stratford Road opposite Cranmore Boulevard.

Knowle
Warwick Road c1965
Knowle, one mile south-east of Solihull, contains a number of interesting old buildings, including the medieval Chester House, and the heavily restored 17th-century Red Lion. This scene looks very quiet, but it wasn't always so. One Sunday in 1945 a tremendous explosion rocked the village, and a ball of flames erupted from behind the trees on Warwick Road. A Mosquito aircraft had crashed after developing engine trouble.

Knowle
The Parish Church c1965
Until the mid 19th century, Knowle was a hamlet within the parish of Hampton-in-Arden. The church, which is now dedicated to St John Baptist, St Lawrence and St Anne, was originally built by Canon Walter Cook as a guild chapel; the Guildhouse can also be seen in the picture. At the Dissolution a petition was raised to save the church on the grounds that Hampton (4 miles south-west) was too far for parishioners to journey to for divine services.

Knowle, Warwick Road c1965 K120017

Knowle, The Parish Church c1965 K120015

KNOWLE, TOP LOCK c1965 K120007

At Knowle a flight of locks raises the canal nearly 42 feet. A flight of five wide locks were built in the 1930s to replace six narrow ones; they can be seen here side-by-side. There are also a number of side ponds here, which date back to the original canal and were built to conserve water.

KNOWLE, GRIMSHAW HALL c1965 K120194

A few hundred yards to the north of Knowle on the road to Hampton-in-Arden stands Grimshaw Hall. Built about 1560, the Hall is noted for its decorative brickwork which features herringbone, lozenge and concave-lozenge patterns, and for its genuine oriel windows on brackets.

Index

Acock's Green 80-81, 82
Aston 56, 57
Bilston 30-31, 32
Birmingham 58-59, 60-61, 62, 63, 64-65, 66, 67, 68, 69, 70, 71
Bournville 72, 73
Brierley Hill 41, 42, 43
Castle Bromwich 54, 55
Chasewater 105, 106
Coventry 89, 90-91, 92, 93, 94-95, 96, 97, 98, 99, 100, 101, 102, 103, 104
Dudley 38-39, 40, 41
Edgbaston 71, 72
Handsworth 57
Harbourne 83, 84-85, 86, 87
King's Norton 74, 75
Kingswinford 53, 54
Knowle 113, 114,
Northfield 76-77, 78, 79
Old Swinford 52, 53
Penn 28
Rednal 88
Sedgeley 37
Shirley 112
Solihull 110, 111
Stourbridge 43, 44-45, 46, 47, 48, 49, 50-51
Sutton Coldfield 106, 107, 108-109, 110
Tettenhall 29
Walsall 33, 34
Wednesbury 35, 36
West Bromwich 36, 37
Willenhall 105
Wolverhampton 18-19, 20-21, 22, 23, 24-25, 26, 27
Yardley 82, 83

Frith Book Co Titles

Frith Book Company publish over a 100 new titles each year. For latest catalogue please contact Frith Book Co.

own Books 96pp, 100 photos. County and Themed Books 128pp, 150 photos (unless specified) All titles hardback laminated case and jacket except those indicated pb (paperback)

Around Barnstaple	1-85937-084-5	£12.99
Around Blackpool	1-85937-049-7	£12.99
Around Bognor Regis	1-85937-055-1	£12.99
Around Bristol	1-85937-050-0	£12.99
Around Cambridge	1-85937-092-6	£12.99
Cheshire	1-85937-045-4	£14.99
Around Chester	1-85937-090-X	£12.99
Around Chesterfield	1-85937-071-3	£12.99

Around Chichester	1-85937-089-6	£12.99
Cornwall	1-85937-054-3	£14.99
Cotswolds	1-85937-099-3	£14.99
Around Derby	1-85937-046-2	£12.99
Devon	1-85937-052-7	£14.99
Dorset	1-85937-075-6	£14.99
Dorset Coast	1-85937-062-4	£14.99
Around Dublin	1-85937-058-6	£12.99
East Anglia	1-85937-059-4	£14.99
Around Eastbourne	1-85937-061-6	£12.99
English Castles	1-85937-078-0	£14.99
Around Falmouth	1-85937-066-7	£12.99
Hampshire	1-85937-064-0	£14.99
Isle of Man	1-85937-065-9	£14.99

Around Maidstone	1-85937-056-X	£12.99
North Yorkshire	1-85937-048-9	£14.99
Around Nottingham	1-85937-060-8	£12.99
Around Penzance	1-85937-069-1	£12.99
Around Reading	1-85937-087-X	£12.99
Around St Ives	1-85937-068-3	£12.99
Around Salisbury	1-85937-091-8	£12.99
Around Scarborough	1-85937-104-3	£12.99
Scottish Castles	1-85937-077-2	£14.99
Around Sevenoaks and Tonbridge	1-85937-057-8	£12.99
Sheffield and S Yorkshire	1-85937-070-5	£14.99
Shropshire	1-85937-083-7	£14.99
Staffordshire	1-85937-047-0 (96pp)	£12.99
Suffolk	1-85937-074-8	£14.99
Surrey	1-85937-081-0	£14.99
Torbay	1-85937-063-2	£12.99
Wiltshire	1-85937-053-5	£14.99

British Life A Century Ago
246 x 189mm 144pp, hardback. Black and white
Lavishly illustrated with photos from the turn of the century, and with extensive commentary. It offers a unique insight into the social history and heritage of bygone Britain.

1-85937-103-5 £17.99

Available from your local bookshop or from the publisher

Frith Book Co Titles Available in 2000

Title	ISBN	Price	Month
Around Bakewell	1-85937-1132	£12.99	Feb
Around Bath	1-85937-097-7	£12.99	Feb
Around Belfast	1-85937-094-2	£12.99	Feb
Around Bournemouth	1-85937-067-5	£12.99	Feb
Cambridgeshire	1-85937-086-1	£14.99	Feb
Essex	1-85937-082-9	£14.99	Feb
Greater Manchester	1-85937-108-6	£14.99	Feb
Around Guildford	1-85937-117-5	£12.99	Feb
Around Harrogate	1-85937-112-4	£12.99	Feb
Hertfordshire	1-85937-079-9	£14.99	Feb
Isle of Wight	1-85937-114-0	£14.99	Feb
Around Lincoln	1-85937-111-6	£12.99	Feb
Margate/Ramsgate	1-85937-116-7	£12.99	Feb
Northumberland and Tyne & Wear	1-85937-072-1	£14.99	Feb
Around Newark	1-85937-105-1	£12.99	Feb
Around Oxford	1-85937-096-9	£12.99	Feb
Oxfordshire	1-85937-076-4	£14.99	Feb
Around Shrewsbury	1-85937-110-8	£12.99	Feb
South Devon Coast	1-85937-107-8	£14.99	Feb
Around Southport	1-85937-106-x	£12.99	Feb
West Midlands	1-85937-109-4	£14.99	Feb
Cambridgeshire	1-85937-086-1	£14.99	Mar
County Durham	1-85937-123-x	£14.99	Mar
Cumbria	1-85937-101-9	£14.99	Mar
Down the Severn	1-85937-118-3	£14.99	Mar
Down the Thames	1-85937-121-3	£14.99	Mar
Around Exeter	1-85937-126-4	£12.99	Mar
Around Folkestone	1-85937-124-8	£12.99	Mar
Gloucestershire	1-85937-102-7	£14.99	Mar
Around Great Yarmouth	1-85937-085-3	£12.99	Mar
Kent Living Memories	1-85937-125-6	£14.99	Mar
Around Leicester	1-85937-073-x	£12.99	Mar
Around Liverpool	1-85937-051-9	£12.99	Mar
Around Plymouth	1-85937-119-1	£12.99	Mar
Around Portsmouth	1-85937-122-1	£12.99	Mar
Around Southampton	1-85937-088-8	£12.99	Mar
Around Stratford upon Avon	1-85937-098-5	£12.99	Mar
Welsh Castles	1-85937-120-5	£14.99	Mar
Canals and Waterways	1-85937-129-9	£17.99	Apr
East Sussex	1-85937-130-2	£14.99	Apr
Exmoor	1-85937-132-9	£14.99	Apr
Farms and Farming	1-85937-134-5	£17.99	Apr
Around Horsham	1-85937-127-2	£12.99	Apr
Ipswich (pb)	1-85937-133-7	£12.99	Apr
Ireland (pb)	1-85937-181-7	£9.99	Apr
London (pb)	1-85937-183-3	£9.99	Apr
New Forest	1-85937-128-0	£14.99	Apr
Scotland	1-85937-182-5	£9.99	Apr
Stone Circles & Ancient Monuments	1-85937-143-4	£17.99	Apr
Sussex (pb)	1-85937-184-1	£9.99	Apr
Colchester (pb)	1-85937-188-4	£8.99	May
County Maps of Britain	1-85937-156-6 (192pp)	£19.99	May
Around Harrow	1-85937-141-8	£12.99	May
Leicestershire (pb)	1-85937-185-x	£9.99	May
Lincolnshire	1-85937-135-3	£14.99	May
Around Newquay	1-85937-140-x	£12.99	May
Nottinghamshire (pb)	1-85937-187-6	£9.99	May
Redhill to Reigate	1-85937-137-x	£12.99	May
Scilly Isles	1-85937-136-1	£14.99	May
Victorian & Edwardian Yorkshire	1-85937-154-x	£14.99	May
Around Winchester	1-85937-139-6	£12.99	May
Yorkshire (pb)	1-85937-186-8	£9.99	May
Berkshire (pb)	1-85937-191-4	£9.99	Jun
Brighton (pb)	1-85937-192-2	£8.99	Jun
Dartmoor	1-85937-145-0	£14.99	Jun
East London	1-85937-080-2	£14.99	Jun
Glasgow (pb)	1-85937-190-6	£8.99	Jun
Kent (pb)	1-85937-189-2	£9.99	Jun
Victorian & Edwardian Kent	1-85937-149-3	£14.99	Jun
North Devon Coast	1-85937-146-9	£14.99	Jun
Peak District	1-85937-100-0	£14.99	Jun
Around Truro	1-85937-147-7	£12.99	Jun
Victorian & Edwardian Maritime Album	1-85937-144-2	£14.99	Jun
West Sussex	1-85937-148-5	£14.99	Jun

Frith Products & Services

Francis Frith would doubtless be pleased to know that the pioneering publishing venture he started in 1860 still continues today. More than a hundred and thirty years later, The Francis Frith Collection continues in the same innovative tradition and is now one of the foremost publishers of vintage photographs in the world. Some of the current activities include:

Interior Decoration

Today Frith's photographs can be seen framed and as giant wall murals in thousands of pubs, restaurants, hotels, banks, retail stores and other public buildings throughout the country. In every case they enhance the unique local atmosphere of the places they depict and provide reminders of gentler days in an increasingly busy and frenetic world.

Product Promotions

Frith products have been used by many major companies to promote the sales of their own products or to reinforce their own history and heritage. Brands include Hovis bread, Courage beers, Scots Porage Oats, Colman's mustard, Cadbury's foods, Mellow Birds coffee, Dunhill pipe tobacco, Guinness, and Bulmer's Cider.

Genealogy and Family History

As the interest in family history and roots grows world-wide, more and more people are turning to Frith's photographs of Great Britain for images of the towns, villages and streets where their ancestors lived; and, of course, photographs of the churches and chapels where their ancestors were christened, married and buried are an essential part of every genealogy tree and family album.
A series of easy-to-use CD Roms is planned for publication, and an increasing number of Frith photographs will be able to be viewed on specialist genealogy sites. A growing range of Frith books will be available on CD.

The Internet

Already thousands of Frith photographs can be viewed and purchased on the internet. By the end of the year 2000 some 60,000 Frith photographs will be available on the internet. The number of sites is constantly expanding, each focussing on different products and services from the Collection.
Some of the sites are listed below.

www.townpages.co.uk
www.icollector.com
www.barclaysquare.co.uk
www.cornwall-online.co.uk

For background information on the Collection look at the two following sites:

www.francisfrith.com
www.francisfrith.co.uk
www.frithbook.co.uk

Frith Products

All Frith photographs are available Framed or just as Mounted Prints, and can be ordered from the address below. From time to time other products - Address Books, Calendars, Table Mats, Postcards etc - are available.

The Frith Collectors' Guild

In response to the many customers who enjoy collecting Frith photographs we have created the Frith Collectors' Guild. Members are entitled to a range of benefits, including a regular magazine, special discounts and special limited edition products.

For further information: if you would like further information on any of the above aspects of the Frith business please contact us at the address below:
The Francis Frith Collection, Frith's Barn, Teffont, Salisbury, Wiltshire England SP3 5QP.
Tel: +44 (0) 1722 716 376 Fax: +44 (0) 1722 716 881 Email: uksales@francisfrith.com

To receive your FREE Mounted Print

Cut out this Voucher and return it with your remittance for £1.50 to cover postage and handling. Choose any photograph included in this book. Your SEPIA print will be A4 in size, and mounted in a cream mount with burgundy rule lines, overall size 14 x 11 inches.

Order additional Mounted Prints at HALF PRICE (only £7.49 each*)

If there are further pictures you would like to order, possibly as gifts for friends and family, acquire them at half price (no additional postage and handling required).

Have your Mounted Prints framed*

For an additional £14.95 per print you can have your chosen Mounted Print framed in an elegant polished wood and gilt moulding, overall size 16 x 13 inches (no additional postage and handling required).

*** IMPORTANT!**
These special prices are only available if ordered using the original voucher on this page (no copies permitted) and at the same time as your free Mounted Print, for delivery to the same address

for FREE and Reduced Price Frith Prints

Picture no.	Page number	Qty	Mounted @ £7.49	Framed + £14.95	Total Cost
		1	**Free of charge***	£	£
			£	£	£
			£	£	£
			£	£	£
			£	£	£
			£	£	£
				* Post & handling	£1.50
Book Title				**Total Order Cost**	**£**

Please do not photocopy this voucher. Only the original is valid, so please cut it out and return it to us.

I enclose a cheque / postal order for £ ....
made payable to 'The Francis Frith Collection'
OR please debit my Mastercard / Visa / Switch / Amex card

Number ....

Expires .... Signature ....

Name Mr/Mrs/Ms ....

Address ....

....

....

....

.... Postcode ....

Daytime Tel No .... Valid to 31/12/01

Frith Collectors' Guild

From time to time we publish a magazine of news and stories about Frith photographs and further special offers of Frith products. If you would like 12 months FREE membership, please return this form.

The Francis Frith Collectors' Guild

Please enrol me as a member for 12 months free of charge.

Name Mr/Mrs/Ms ....

Address ....

....

....

.... Postcode ....

Send completed forms to:
The Francis Frith Collection, Frith's Barn, Teffont, Salisbury, Wiltshire SP3 5QP